Personal
Decisions
in the
Public
Square

D0209892

Personal
Decisions
in the
Public
Square

Beyond Problem Solving into
a Positive Sociology

Robert A. Stebbins

Transaction Publishers
New Brunswick (U.S.A.) and London (U.K.)

Library of Congress Catalog Number: 2008030990
ISBN: 978-1-4128-0826-2
Printed in the United States of America

Library of Congress Cataloging-in-Publication

Stebbins, Robert A., 1938-
Personal decision in the public square : beyond problem solving into a
   positive sociology / Robert A. Stebbins.
        p. cm.
   Includes bibliographical references and index.
   ISBN 978-1-4128-0826-2 (alk. paper)
   1. Self-realization. 2. Satisfaction. 3. Quality of life. 4. Leisure.
   5. Work. 6. Sociology. I. Title.

BF637.S4S74   2008
302'.1—dc22   2008030990

To Karin

Contents

List of Tables and Figures

Preface

"Positive sociology" is my label for the new scholarly field described in this book. It looks into how, why, and when people pursue those things in life that they desire, the things they do to make their existence attractive and worth living. Positive sociology is the study of what people do to organize their lives such that those lives become, in combination, substantially rewarding, satisfying, and fulfilling.

This new field differs from the discipline's mainstream, which is predominantly problem-centered. That is, a large segment of sociology has focused and continues to focus on explaining and ameliorating various problematic aspects of life, aspects many people dislike because they make their lives disagreeable. But, for most people in Western society, there is much more to life than eliminating or adequately controlling crime, drug addiction, urban pollution, daily stress, domestic violence, overpopulation, and so on. To be sure, significant levels of success in these areas bring a noticeable measure of tranquility to people substantially affected by them, but they do not, in themselves, generate positiveness in daily life, only relief, tranquility, security, and similar feelings.

Compared with the mainstream this new field must, of necessity, start from some different premises. In general explaining positiveness rests on a nonproblematic model. That is, the principal wellspring of positive sociology is, in large part, the sociology of leisure, a field I recently portrayed as the "happy science" because of its central focus on the attractive side of life (Stebbins, 2007c). Among the basic concepts in the sociology of leisure, and hence in positive sociology, are activity and human agency. An *activity* is a type of pursuit wherein participants mentally or physically (often both) think or do something, motivated by the hope of achieving a desired end. Though not all our activities are positive (e.g., going through airport security, paying income taxes), it appears most are. The centrality of positive activity in this new field is one of its hallmarks and one of the premises separating it from other sociological specialties. The concept of *agency*—personal action taken to reach a goal – is also key to positive sociology, which unlike activity however, is also a crucial idea in some other areas of the social sciences.

Positive sociology centers on the leisure domain of life and its main conceptual roots here are also found in the approach known as the serious leisure perspective. This theoretic framework synthesizes the three main forms of leisure (serious, casual, and project-based) showing, at once, their distinctive features, similarities, and interrelationships. Notwithstanding the importance of leisure, positive sociology must also consider the two other domains of life: work and nonwork obligation. For they bear enormously on the quest for balance in our routine pursuit of well-being as carried on against the disagreeable requirements found in these two domains.

Leisure, activity, human agency, and the other concepts of positive sociology do not exist in a vacuum. In broad terms, this new field is framed and to some extent simultaneously both constrained and facilitated by two sets of conditions: personal and social. The personal conditions include health, wealth, marital status, level of education, taste and talent for a given activity, knowledge of activities, and the like. Numbering among the social conditions are historical forces, type of government, local and national culture, gender stereotype, ethnicity (including religion, race, nationality), educational system, geographic location, and others. The problem-centered interests mentioned earlier may be conceived of, in broad terms, as oriented toward particular constellations of social conditions. There is no doubt that pursuit of positive activities directed by human agency is, at once, framed, constrained, and facilitated by these diverse forces. Nor is there doubt that a positive sociology will also have to account for the three processes of framing, constraining, and facilitating.

In short the social and personal conditions in which positiveness is embedded are as much a part of positive sociology as the central propositions just referred to. At various points in this book I tie these propositions to a number of the personal and social conditions that bear on their validity. In this manner, I hope to bridge the micro-macro divide that, more often than not, attenuates full sociological explanation of phenomena, a split that should never be allowed to prevail in this new positive branch and thereby hinder its maximum development.

My object in this book is to show the grand lines of what a positive sociology should look like. Still, in a pioneering effort as expansive as this, it is certainly possible that I have missed one or more important ideas, dimensions, theoretic frameworks, or personal and social conditions that should have been included. I apologize for any such omissions, but want to encourage all who take seriously the contents of this treatise to see them as opportunities to contribute to the new field, whether they do this through research, theoretic elaboration, or debate on key premises. Like Rome, an intellectual entity as broad and different as this one cannot be fully set out in one swoop.

Meanwhile, for those people—be they research scientists or the lay public—who would like to deepen their understanding of how to make their own lives and those of others more attractive, more worth living, and to understand why, positive sociology offers some answers.

Acknowledgements

Teresa Freire of the University of Minho in Portugal had the essence of a positive social science in mind when she invited me to address a plenary session of the Third European Congress on Positive Psychology held there in July, 2006. The title of my talk—"The Serious Leisure Perspective and Positive Psychology"—shows how I chose to introduce leisure to this relatively new branch of psychology. When I received the invitation to make this presentation, it was necessary, before accepting it, to find out what positive psychology is. At first, visions of logical positivism and the Vienna School danced in my head, although they were quickly discarded as I learned about positive psychology from a website and from articles on the subject written by Martin Seligman, its prime mover. Seligman, a psychologist, advised that every social science should be moving beyond its dominant, problem-centered approach to also examine systematically the positive aspects of social and psychological life falling within its purview. It was immediately clear to me that such advice applied with equal force to sociology. With this realization the idea for the present volume was born.

Lawrence Downes published in the 16 June 2008 online edition of the New York Times a short article written as an elegy for copy editors. In treating of the important service they perform in the newspaper business, he observed that "they untangle twisted prose. They are surgeons, removing growths of error and irrelevance; they are minimalist chefs, straining fat." This job description applies equally to copy editors working on books, and in particular, to the work of Laurence Mintz who worked on the present volume. This is my third publication with Transaction, and he has masterfully untangled, removed, and strained questionable prose in all three. Thanks again Larry.

1

Three Domains of Activity

"He enjoys true leisure who has time to improve his soul's estate."
—*Henry David Thoreau*

This book explores how, when, where, and why people pursue those things in life that they desire, the things they do to create a worthwhile existence that is, in combination, substantially rewarding, satisfying, and fulfilling. In the following pages I set out a positive sociology, which joins with the new field of positive psychology to follow its interest in uncovering people's strengths and promoting their positive functioning (Snyder & Lopez, 2007, p. 3). As a complement to this branch of psychology, however, positive sociology centers on social meanings, interpersonal interaction, human agency, and the personal and social conditions in which these three unfold with reference to particular human activities. It centers on what people can do and want to do to make their lives worth living. This is a book about positive sociology, which acknowledges, however, a significant intellectual debt to its counterpart in psychology. Chapters 4 and 5 attest its importance for the kind of sociology presented here.

"Positive sociology," as defined here, is a new idea, even if traces of it have been around as long as sociology itself. Remember, for instance, that Max Weber (1947, pp. 413-415) wrote on amateurs. Robert Dubin (1979, p. 405), writing more recently at a time when "relevance" was the reigning battle cry in American sociology, observed that a relevant sociology should do more than focus on the "disarticulations between the individual and society." He said it also needs theoretic models on how people construct "worthwhile lives." Such models, this book will stress, are predominantly the province of the sociology of leisure, the principal wellspring of positive sociology. Unfortunately for positive sociology, the sociology of leisure has been, throughout the history of its parent discipline, a marginal branch (Stebbins, 2006, p. xiii). In the present volume, I argue that sociology must become positive; that is it must recognize the central place of the pursuit of those (mostly leisure) activities that make life rewarding, satisfying, and fulfilling, though in doing so, I also argue that it should certainly not abandon its longstanding interest in trying to understand and solve life's many difficult social problems, its disarticulations.

A positive sociology, if it is to plow any significant, new intellectual ground, must start, in good measure, from premises different from those of mainstream, problem-centered sociology. That is, a large segment of sociology has focused and continues to focus on explaining and handling the various problematic aspects of life that many people dislike, that make their lives disagreeable (see also Jeffries et al, 2006). Controlling or even ameliorating these problems, to the extent this is truly effective, brings welcome relief to those people. Still managing a community problem in this way, be the problem rampant drug addiction, growing domestic violence, persistent poverty, or enduring labor conflict, is not the same as people pursuing something they like. Instead, control of, or solutions to, these problems, bring, in effect, a level of tranquility to life – these efforts make life less disagreeable. This, in turn, gives those who benefit from them some time, energy, and inclination to search for what will now make their existence more agreeable, more worth living.

In other words, there is second major step to take, which is to find the positive, rewarding side of life, made possible after having accomplished the first major step of eliminating or at least controlling as much as possible, those conditions that undermine our basic tranquility. It is in this sense that much of sociology over the years can be said to have concentrated on the negative to the neglect, if not the detriment, of the positive. Nevertheless let me be clear that I am in no way arguing that positiveness is completely absent during the first step. For, obviously, some people manage to pursue leisure and other attractive aspects of life, at times quite effectively, while numerous social problems rage about them. That is not my point. Instead I want to underscore sociology's general neglect of the second step, including when it overlaps— as it indeed usual does—the first step.[1]

Still the control and solution of problems are complex processes. Some people pursue as leisure their contribution to the amelioration of certain social issues. Examples include volunteering to serve food to the needy, mentor juvenile delinquents, read to hospital patients, clean up beaches, and provide water filters and electrical lighting to

Third World countries. Positive sociology recognizes these activities as leisure pursuits, whereas problem-oriented sociology tends to ignore the attractive, agreeable side of such pursuits. Instead the second favors study, control, and amelioration of the problems themselves, commonly referred to without reference to the volunteer component as poverty, juvenile delinquency, health care, environmental pollution, and Third World underdevelopment, respectively.

Moreover, many people face problems while trying to organize their leisure lives. We may refer to these as "positive problems," in that controlling, or solving them, helps clear the road for positiveness in everyday life. Consider two examples: the wife who persuades her husband to prepare evening meals, thereby freeing her for community theater rehearsals; and the father who reorganizes his volunteering at the food bank around the new schedule of soccer practices of his young children. Dealing with such problems is the province of positive sociology, not its problem-centered counterpart.

The distinctive premises of the positive sociology proposed in this book root primarily in the sociology of leisure, which are, however, expanded to apply to a larger swath of everyday life. That is, at the *activity* level, all of everyday life may be conceptualized as being experienced in one of three domains: work, leisure, and non-work obligation. One might ask at this point if our existence is not more complicated than this. Indeed it is, for each of the three is itself enormously complex, and there is also some overlap in the domains. The novel claim of this book – that sociology can be, and should also be, positive and that positive attitudes and activities matter a great deal—rests on this, the domain approach. Considering the domain of non-work obligation, emphasizing the positive side of work, and viewing both from the angle of leisure and positiveness, brings to sociology, anthropology, and psychology an uncommon orientation toward understanding contemporary life.

As argued above, the pursuit of activities in these three domains is framed in a wide range of social conditions, some of which, at that level of analysis, blur domainal boundaries. For example, if the state mandates that no one may work more than thirty-five hours a week, this will affect the typical amount of time spent in activities in the work domain vis-à-vis those in the domains of leisure and non-work obligation. Or consider the condition of poverty. For the impoverished its components of hunger, disease, malnutrition, and unemployment largely efface the non-work and leisure domains, forcing these people into the full-time activity of survival (subsistence-level work). Third, on the cultural plane, some groups (e.g., religious, communal) stress the importance of altruism and its expression in volunteering. Volunteering here is leisure activity, which however, loses this quality when experienced as coercion. The feeling of *having* to "volunteer" transforms such activity into a kind of non-work obligation. Examples of this nature are found throughout this book; they constitute a mechanism for facilitating understanding of the positive activities of life from the angle of the relevant social and personal conditions framing them.

Before considering the three domains, however, we must look at another important idea common all three: activity.

Activity and Role

In positive sociology an *activity* is a type of pursuit, wherein participants in it mentally or physically (often both) think or do something, motivated by the hope of achieving a desired end. Life is filled with activities, both pleasant and unpleasant: sleeping, mowing the lawn, taking the train to work, having a tooth filled, eating lunch, playing tennis matches, running a meeting, and on and on. Activities, as this list illustrates, may be categorized as work, leisure, or non-work obligation. They are, furthermore, general. In some instances, they refer to the behavioral side of recognizable roles, for example commuter, tennis player, and chair of a meeting. In others we may recognize the activity but not conceive of it so formally as a role, exemplified in someone sleeping, mowing a lawn, or eating lunch (not as patron in a restaurant).

The concept of activity is an abstraction, and as such, is broader than that of role. In other words, roles are associated with particular statuses, or positions, in society, whereas with activities, some are status based while others are not. For instance, sleeper is not a status, even if sleeping is an activity. It is likewise with lawn mower (person). Sociologists, anthropologists, and psychologists tend to see social relations in terms of roles, and as a result, overlook activities whether aligned with a role or not. Meanwhile certain important parts of life consist of engaging in activities not recognized as roles. Where would many of us be could we not routinely sleep or eat lunch?

Moreover, another dimension separates role and activity, namely, that of statics and dynamics. Roles are static whereas activities are dynamic.[2] Roles, classically conceived of, are relatively inactive expectations for behavior, whereas in activities, people are actually behaving, mentally or physically thinking or doing things to achieve certain ends. This dynamic quality provides a powerful explanatory link between an activity and a person's motivation to participate in it. Nevertheless, the idea of role *is* useful in positive sociology, since participants do encounter role expectations in certain activities (e.g., those in sport, work, volunteering). Although the concept of activity does not include these expectations, in its dynamism, it can, much more effectively than role, account for invention and human agency.

This definition of activity gets further refined in the concept of *core activity*: a distinctive set of interrelated actions or steps that must be followed to achieve the outcome or product that the participant seeks. As with general activities core activities are pursued in work, leisure, and non-work obligation. Consider some examples in serious leisure: a core activity of alpine skiing is descending snow-covered slopes, in cabinet making it is shaping and finishing wood, and in volunteer fire fighting is putting out blazes and rescuing people from them. In each case, the participant takes several interrelated steps to successfully ski down hill, make a cabinet, or rescue someone. In casual leisure core activities, which are much less complex than in serious leisure, are exemplified in the actions required to hold sociable conversations with friends, savor beautiful scenery, and offer simple volunteer services (e.g., handing out leaflets, directing traffic in a theater parking lot, clearing snow off the neighborhood hockey rink). Work-related core activities are seen in, for instance, the actions of a surgeon during an operation or the improvisations on a melody by a jazz clarinetist. The core activity in mowing a lawn (non-work obligation) is pushing or riding the mower. Executing an attractive core activity and its component steps and actions is a main feature drawing participants to the general activity encompassing it, because this core directly enables them to reach a cherished goal. It is the opposite for disagreeable core activities. In short the core activity has motivational value of its own, even if more strongly held for some activities than others and even if some activities are disagreeable but still have to be done.

Core activities can be classified as simple or complex, the two concepts finding their place at opposite poles of a continuum. The location of a core activity on this continuum partially explains its appeal or lack thereof. Most casual leisure is comprised of a set of simple core activities. Here *homo otiosus* (leisure man) need only turn on the television set, observe the scenery, drink the glass of wine (no oenophile he), or gossip about someone. Complexity in casual leisure increases slightly when playing a board game using dice, participating in a Hash House Harrier treasure hunt, or serving as a casual volunteer by, say, collecting bottles for the

Scouts or making tea and coffee after a religious service. And Harrison's (2001) study of upper-middle-class Canadian mass tourists revealed a certain level of complexity in their sensual experience of the touristic sites they visited. For people craving the simple things in life, this is the kind of leisure to head for. The other two domains abound with equivalent simple core activities, as in the work of a parking lot attendant (receiving cash/making change) or the efforts of a householder whose non-work obligation of the day is raking leaves.

So, if complexity is what people want, they must look elsewhere. Leisure projects are necessarily more complex than casual leisure activities. The types of projects listed later in this chapter provide, I believe, ample proof of that. Nonetheless, they are not nearly as complex as the core activities around which serious leisure revolves. The accumulated knowledge, skill, training, and experience of, for instance, the amateur trumpet player, hobbyist stamp collector, and volunteer emergency medical worker are vast, and defy full description of how they are applied during conduct of the core activity. Of course, neophytes in the serious leisure activities lack these acquisitions, though it is unquestionably their intention to acquire them to a level where they will feel fulfilled. As with simple core activities complex equivalents also exist in the other two domains. Examples in work include the two earlier examples of the surgeon and jazz clarinetist. In the non-work domain, two examples considered later in this chapter are more or less complex: driving in city traffic and (for some people) preparing their annual income tax return.

Can all of life be characterized as an endless unfolding of activities? Probably not. For instance the definition of activity does not fit things some people are, through violence, compelled to experience entirely against their will, including rape, torture, interrogation, forced feeding, and judicial execution. It would seem to be likewise for the actions of those driven by a compulsive mental disorder. There are also comparatively more benign situations in which most people still feel compelled to participate, among them, enduring receipt of a roadside traffic citation or a bawling out from the boss. Both fail to qualify as activities. In all these examples the ends sought are those of other people, as they pursue their activities. Meanwhile the "victims" lack agency, unless they can manage to counterattack with an activity of resistance.

Activity as just defined is, by and large, a foreign idea in psychology, anthropology, and sociology. Certainly scholars in those fields sometimes talk about, for instance, criminal, political, or economic activity, but in so doing, they are referring, in general terms, to a broad category of behavior, not a particular set of actions comprising a pursuit. Instead, our positive sociological concept of activity knows its greatest currency in the interdisciplinary fields of leisure studies and physical education and, more recently, kinesiology. And I suspect that the first adopted the idea from the second. There has always been, in physical education, discussion of and research on activities promoting conditioning, exercise, outdoor interests, human movement, and the like.

The activity, sometimes joined with role, most of the time agreeable, but sometimes disagreeable, is the cornerstone of a positive sociology. The idea is eminently sociological, since many activities, in this way or that, involve the participant with other people while unfolding in particular social conditions. It is through certain activities that people, propelled by their own agency, find positive things in life, which they blend and balance with certain negative things they must also deal with.

All this is carried out in the three previously mentioned domains. Because my intellectual, and scientific background for writing about positive sociology was acquired in the study of what people do in their free time, radiating from there to work and later to non-work obligation, I will discuss the three domains in that order.

The Serious Leisure Perspective

The serious leisure perspective may be described, in simplest terms, as the theoretic framework that synthesizes three main forms of leisure showing, at once, their distinctive features, similarities, and interrelationships.[3] Additionally the Perspective (wherever Perspective appears as shorthand for serious leisure perspective, to avoid confusion, the first letter will be capitalized) considers how the three forms—serious leisure, casual leisure, and project-based leisure – are shaped by various psychological, social, cultural, and historical conditions. Each form serves as a conceptual umbrella for a range of types of related activities. That the Perspective takes its name from the first of these should, in no way, suggest that I regard it, in some abstract sense, as the most important or superior of the three. Rather the Perspective is so titled, simply because it got its start in the study of serious leisure; such leisure is, strictly from the standpoint of intellectual invention, the godfather of the other two. Furthermore serious leisure has become the bench mark from which analyses of casual and project-based leisure have often been undertaken. So naming the Perspective after the first facilitates intellectual recognition; it keeps the idea in familiar territory for all concerned.

My research findings and theoretic musings have nevertheless evolved and coalesced into a typological map of the world of leisure. That is, so far as known at present, all leisure (at least in Western society) can be classified according to one of the three forms and their several types and subtypes. More precisely the serious leisure perspective offers a classification and explanation of all leisure activities and experiences, as these two are framed in the social psychological, social, cultural, and historical conditions in which each activity and accompanying experience take place. Figure 1.1 portrays the typological structure of the Perspective.

What is Leisure?

Scientifically speaking, leisure may be defined as uncoerced activity undertaken during free time. Uncoerced activity is positive activity that, using their abilities and resources, people both want to do and can do at either a personally satisfying or a deeper fulfilling level (Stebbins, 2005a;

Figure 1.1
The Serious Leisure Perspective

Source: http://www.soci.ucalgary.ca/seriousleisure

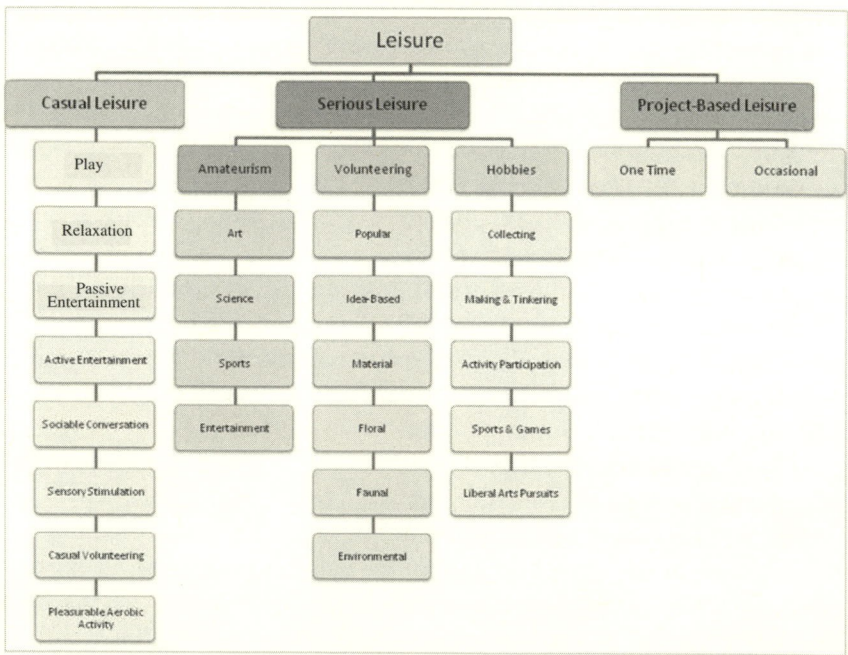

Diagram formulated by Jenna Hartel

2006, pp. 4-5). Later in this book we will consider the place of boredom in everyday life. Let us note for the moment, however, that boredom occurring in free time *is* an uncoerced state, even while it is not something that bored people *want* to experience. Therefore, it is not leisure; it is not a positive experience, as just defined. In fact any activity may be boring, be it free time, work, or non-work obligation. In these circumstances the desired end and the means to it are uninspiring. In free time the boring activity (e.g., hanging out on a street corner with nothing else to do, watching uninteresting television) is commonly the only activity seen by participants as available to them.

Uncoerced, people in leisure believe they are doing something they are not pushed to do, something they are not disagreeably obliged to do. In this definition emphasis is ipso facto on the acting individual and the play of human agency. This in no way denies that there may be things people want to do but cannot do because of any number of constraints on choice, because of limiting social and personal conditions; for example, aptitude, ability, socialized leisure tastes, knowledge of available activities, and accessibility of activities. In other words, when using this definition of leisure, whose central ingredient is lack of coercion, we must be sure to understand leisure activities in relation to their larger personal, structural, cultural, and historical background. And it follows that leisure is not really freely chosen, as some observers have claimed (e.g., Parker, 1983, pp. 8-9; Kelly, 1990, p. 7), since choice of activity is significantly shaped by this background.

Serious Leisure

Serious leisure is the systematic pursuit of an amateur, hobbyist, or volunteer activity sufficiently substantial, interesting, and fulfilling for the participant to find a (leisure) career there acquiring and expressing a combination of its special skills, knowledge, and experience. I coined the term (Stebbins, 1982) to express the way the people he interviewed and observed viewed the importance of these three kinds of activity in their everyday lives. The adjective "serious" (a word my research respondents often used) embodies such qualities as earnestness, sincerity, importance, and carefulness, rather than gravity, solemnity, joylessness, distress, and anxiety. Although the second set of terms occasionally describes serious leisure events, they are uncharacteristic of them and fail to nullify, or, in many cases, even dilute, the overall fulfillment gained by the participants. The idea of "career" in this definition follows sociological tradition, where careers are seen as available in all substantial, complex roles, including those in leisure. Finally, as we shall see shortly, serious leisure is distinct from casual leisure and project-based leisure.

Amateurs are found in art, science, sport, and entertainment, where they are invariably linked in a variety of ways with professional counterparts. The two can be distinguished descriptively in that the activity in question constitutes a livelihood for professionals but not amateurs. Furthermore, most professionals work full time at the activity whereas all amateurs pursue it part time. The part-time professionals in art and entertainment complicate this picture; although they work part time, their work is judged by other professionals and by the amateurs as of professional quality. Amateurs and professionals are locked in and therefore defined by a system of relations linking them and their publics—the "professional-amateur-public (P-A-P) system" (discussed in more detail in Stebbins, 1979; 1992, chap. 3; 2006, pp. 6-8).

Hobbyists lack this professional alter ego, suggesting that, historically, all amateurs were hobbyists before their fields professionalized. Both types are drawn to their leisure pursuits significantly more by self-interest than by altruism, whereas volunteers engage in activities requiring a more or less equal blend of these two motives. Hobbyists may be classified in five types: collectors, makers and tinkerers, noncompetitive activity participants (e.g., fishing, hiking, orienteering), hobbyist sports and games (e.g., ultimate Frisbee, croquet, gin rummy), and the liberal arts hobbies (primarily reading in an area of history, science, philosophy, literature, etc., see Stebbins, 1994).

Smith, Stebbins and Dover (2006: pp. 239-240) define *volunteer* – whether economic or volitional—as someone who performs, even for a short period of time, volunteer work in either an informal or a formal setting. It is through volunteer work that this person provides a service or benefit to one or more individuals (they must be outside that person's family), usually receiving no pay, even though people serving in volunteer programs are sometimes compensated for out-of-pocket expenses. Moreover, in the field of nonprofit studies, since no volunteer work is involved, giving (of, say, blood, money, clothing), as an altruistic act, is not considered volunteering. Meanwhile, in the typical case, volunteers who are altruistically providing a service or benefit to others are themselves also benefiting from various rewards experienced during this process (e.g., pleasant social interaction, self-enriching experiences, sense of contributing to nonprofit group success). In other words volunteering is motivated by two basic attitudes: altruism *and* self-interest.

The conception of volunteering that squares best with a positive sociology revolves, in significant part, around a central subjective motivational question: it must be determined whether volunteers feel they are engaging in an enjoyable (casual leisure), fulfilling (serious leisure), or enjoyable or fulfilling (project-based leisure) core activity that they have had the option to accept or reject on their own terms. A key element in the leisure conception of volunteering is the felt absence of coercion, moral or otherwise, to participate in the volunteer activity (Stebbins, 1996c), an element that, in "marginal volunteering" (Stebbins, 2001b) may be experienced in degrees, as more or less coercive. The reigning conception of volunteering in nonprofit sector research is not that of volunteering as leisure, but rather volunteering as unpaid work. The first—an *economic* conception—defines volunteering as the absence of payment as livelihood, whether in money or in kind. This definition, for the most part, leaves unanswered the messy question of motivation so crucial to the second, positive sociological, definition, which is a *volitional* conception.

Volitionally speaking, volunteer activities are motivated, in part, by one of six types of interest: interest in activities involving (1) people; (2) ideas; (3) things; (4) flora; (5) fauna; or (6) the natural environment (Stebbins, 2007b). Each type, or combination of types, offers its volunteers an opportunity to pursue, through an altruistic activity, a particular kind of interest. Thus, volunteers interested in working with certain ideas are attracted to idea-based volunteering, while those interested in certain kinds of animals are attracted to faunal volunteering. Interest forms the first dimension of a typology of volunteers and volunteering.

But, since volunteers and volunteering cannot be explained by interest alone, a second dimension is needed. This is supplied by the serious leisure perspective and its three forms. This perspective, as already noted, sets out the motivational and contextual (socio-cultural, historical) foundation of the three. The intersections of these two dimensions produce eighteen types of volunteers and volunteering, exemplified in idea-based serious leisure volunteers, material casual leisure volunteering (working with things), and environmental project-based volunteering (see table 1.1)

Serious leisure is further defined by six distinctive qualities, qualities uniformly found among its amateurs, hobbyists, and volunteers. One is the occasional need to *persevere*. Participants who want to continue experiencing the same level of fulfillment in the activity have to meet certain challenges from time to time. Thus, musicians must practice assiduously to

Table 1.1
A Leisure-Based Theoretic Typology of Volunteers and Volunteering

Leisure Form	Type of Volunteer		
	Serious Leisure (SL)	Casual Leisure (CL)	Project-Based Leisure (PBL)
Popular	SL Popular	CL Popular	PBL Popular
Idea-Based	SL Idea-Based	CL Idea-Based	PBL Idea-Based
Material	SL Material	CL Material	PBL Material
Floral	SL Floral	CL Floral	PBL Floral
Faunal	SL Faunal	CL Faunal	PBL Faunal
Environmental	SL Environmental	CL Environmental	PBL Environmental

master difficult musical passages, baseball players must throw repeatedly to perfect favorite pitches, and volunteers must search their imaginations for new approaches with which to help children with reading problems. It happens in all three types of serious leisure that deepest fulfillment sometimes comes at the end of the activity rather than during it, from sticking with it through thick and thin, from conquering adversity.

Another quality distinguishing all three types of serious leisure is the opportunity to follow a (leisure) *career* in the endeavor, a career shaped by its own special contingencies, turning points, and stages of achievement and involvement. A career that, in some fields notably certain arts and sports may nevertheless include decline. Moreover, most, if not all, careers here owe their existence to a third quality: serious leisure participants make significant personal *effort* using their specially acquired knowledge, training, or skill and, indeed at times, all three. Careers for serious leisure participants unfold along lines of their efforts to achieve, for instance, a high level of showmanship, athletic prowess, or scientific knowledge or to accumulate formative experiences in a volunteer role.

Serious leisure is further distinguished by numerous *durable benefits*, or tangible, salutary outcomes such activity for its participants. They are self-actualization, self-enrichment, self-expression, regeneration or renewal of self, feelings of accomplishment, enhancement of self-image, social interaction and sense of belonging, and lasting physical products of the activity (e.g., a painting, scientific paper, piece of furniture). A further benefit—self-gratification, or pure fun, which is by far the most evanescent benefit in this list—is also enjoyed by casual leisure participants. The possibility of realizing such benefits constitutes a powerful goal in serious leisure.

Fifth, serious leisure is distinguished by a unique *ethos* that emerges in parallel with each expression of it. An ethos is the spirit of the community of serious leisure participants, as manifested in shared attitudes, practices, values, beliefs, goals, and so on. The social world of the participants is the organizational milieu in which the associated ethos – at bottom a cultural formation—is expressed (as attitudes, beliefs, values) or realized (as practices, goals). According to Unruh (1979; 1980) every social world has its characteristic groups, events, routines, practices, and organizations. It is held together, to an important degree, by semiformal, or mediated, communication. In other words, in the typical case, social worlds are neither heavily bureaucratized nor substantially organized through intense face-to-face interaction. Rather, communication is commonly mediated by newsletters, posted notices, telephone messages, mass mailings, radio and television announcements, and similar means.

The social world is a diffuse, amorphous entity to be sure, but nevertheless one of great importance in the impersonal, segmented life of the modern urban community. Its importance is further amplified by a parallel element of the special ethos, which is missing from Unruh's conception, namely that such worlds are also constituted of a rich subculture. One function of this subculture is to interrelate the many components of this diffuse and amorphous entity. In other words, there is associated with each social world a set of special norms, values, beliefs, styles, moral principles, performance standards, and similar shared representations.

The sixth quality—participants in serious leisure tend to identify strongly with their chosen pursuits—springs from the presence of the other five distinctive qualities. In contrast, most casual leisure, although not usually humiliating or despicable, is nonetheless too fleeting, mundane, and commonplace to become the basis for a distinctive *identity* for most people.

Motivation

Furthermore certain rewards and costs come with pursuing a hobbyist, amateur, or volunteer activity. Both implicitly and explicitly much of serious leisure theory rests on the following proposition: to understand the meaning of such leisure for those who pursue it is in significant part to understand their motivation for the pursuit. Moreover, one fruitful approach to understanding the motives that lead to serious leisure participation is to study them through the eyes of the participants who, past studies reveal (Stebbins, 1992, chap. 6; 1996a; 1998b; Arai & Pedlar, 1997), see it as a mix of offsetting costs and rewards experienced in the central activity. The rewards of this activity tend to outweigh the costs, however, the result being that the participants usually find a high level of personal fulfilment in them.

The rewards of a serious leisure pursuit are the more or less routine values that attract and hold its enthusiasts.[4] Every serious leisure career both frames and is framed by the continuous search for these rewards, a search that takes months, and in some fields years, before the participant consistently finds deep satisfaction in his or her amateur, hobbyist, or volunteer role. Ten rewards have so far emerged in the course of my various exploratory studies of amateurs, hobbyists, and career volunteers. As the following list shows, the rewards are predominantly personal.

Personal rewards

1. Personal enrichment (cherished experiences)
2. Self-actualization (developing skills, abilities, knowledge)
3. Self-expression (expressing skills, abilities, knowledge already developed)
4. Self-image (known to others as a particular kind of serious leisure participant)
5. Self-gratification (combination of superficial enjoyment and deep fulfillment)
6. Re-creation (regeneration) of oneself through serious leisure after a day's work
7. Financial return (from a serious leisure activity)

Social rewards

8. Social attraction (associating with other serious leisure participants, with clients as a volunteer, participating in the social world of the activity)
9. Group accomplishment (group effort in accomplishing a serious leisure project; senses of helping, being needed, being altruistic)
10. Contribution to the maintenance and development of the group (including senses of helping, being needed, being altruistic in making the contribution)

Further, every serious leisure activity contains its own costs—a distinctive combination of tensions, dislikes and disappointments—which each participant confronts in his or her special way. Tensions and dislikes develop within the activity or through its imperfect mesh with work, family, and other leisure interests. Put more precisely, the goal of gaining fulfillment in serious leisure is the drive to experience the rewards of a given leisure activity, such that its costs are seen by the participant as more or less insignificant by comparison. This is at once the meaning of the activity for the participant and that person's motivation for engaging in it. It is this motivational sense of the concept of reward that distinguishes it from the idea of durable benefit set out earlier, an idea that emphasizes outcomes rather than antecedent conditions.

Nonetheless, the two ideas constitute two sides of the same social psychological coin. Moreover, this brief discussion shows that some positive psychological states may be founded, to some extent, on particular negative, often noteworthy, conditions (e.g., tennis elbow, frostbite [cross-country skiing], stage fright, frustration [in acquiring a collectable, learning a part]). Such conditions can make the senses of achievement and self-fulfillment even more pronounced as the enthusiast manages to conquer adversity.

Thrills and Psychological Flow

Thrills are part of this reward system. *Thrills*, or high points, are the sharply exciting events and occasions that stand out in the minds of those who pursue a kind of serious leisure or devotee work. In general, they tend to be associated with the rewards of self-enrichment and, to a lesser extent, those of self-actualization and self-expression. That is, thrills in serious leisure and devotee work may be seen as situated manifestations of certain more abstract rewards; they are what participants in some fields seek as concrete expressions of the rewards they find there. They are important, in substantial part, because they motivate the participant to stick with the pursuit in hope of finding similar experiences again and again and because they demonstrate that diligence and commitment may pay off. Because thrills, as defined here, are based on a certain level of mastery of a core activity, they know no equivalent in casual leisure. The thrill of a roller coaster ride is qualitatively different from a successful descent down roaring rapids in a kayak where the boater has the experience, knowledge, and skill to accomplish this.

Over the years I have identified a number of thrills that come with the serious leisure activities I studied. These thrills are exceptional instances of the *flow* experience. Thus, although the idea of flow originated with the work of Mihalyi Csikszentmihalyi (1990), and has therefore an intellectual history quite separate from that of serious leisure, it does nevertheless happen, depending on the activity, that it is a key motivational force there. For example I found flow was highly prized in the hobbies of kayaking, mountain/ice climbing, and snowboarding (Stebbins, 2005b). What then is flow?

The intensity with which some participants approach their leisure suggests that, there, they may at times be in psychological flow. Flow, a form of optimal experience, is possibly the most widely discussed and studied generic intrinsic reward in the psychology of work and leisure. Although many types of work and leisure generate little or no flow for their participants, those that do are found primarily the "devotee occupations" (discussed in the section on work) and serious leisure. Still, it appears that each work and leisure activity capable of producing flow does so in terms unique to it. And it follows that each of these activities, especially their core activities, must be carefully studied to discover the properties contributing to the distinctive flow experience it offers.

In his theory of optimal experience, Csikszentmihalyi (1990, pp. 3-5, 54) describes and explains the psychological foundation of the many flow activities in work and leisure, as exemplified in chess, dancing, surgery, and rock climbing. Flow is "autotelic" experience, or the sensation that comes with the actual enacting of intrinsically rewarding activity. Over the years, Csikszentmihalyi (1990, pp. 49-67) has identified and explored eight components of this experience. It is easy to see how this quality of complex core activity, when present, is sufficiently rewarding and, it follows, highly valued to endow it with many of the qualities of serious leisure, thereby rendering the two, at the motivational level, inseparable in several ways. And this holds even though most people tend to think of work and leisure as vastly different. The eight components are

1. Sense of competence in executing the activity;
2. Requirement of concentration;
3. Clarity of goals of the activity;
4. Immediate feedback from the activity;
5. Sense of deep, focused involvement in the activity;
6. Sense of control in completing the activity;
7. Loss of self-consciousness during the activity;
8. Sense of time is truncated during the activity.

These components are self-evident, except possibly for the first and the sixth. With reference to the first, flow fails to develop when the activity is either too easy or too difficult; to experience flow the participant must feel capable of performing a moderately challenging activity. The sixth component refers to the perceived degree of control the participant has over execution of the activity. This is not a matter of personal competence; rather it is one of degree of maneuverability in the fact of uncontrollable external forces, a condition well illustrated in situations faced by the mountain hobbyists mentioned above, as when the water level suddenly rises on the river or an unpredicted snowstorm results in a whiteout on a mountain snowboard slope. Viewed from the serious leisure perspective, psychological flow tends to be associated with the rewards of self-enrichment and, to a lesser extent, those of self-actualization and self-expression.

Casual Leisure

Casual leisure is immediately intrinsically rewarding, relatively short-lived pleasurable activity requiring little or no special training to enjoy it. It is fundamentally hedonic, pursued for its significant level of pure enjoyment, or pleasure. The termed was coined by the author in the 1982 conceptual statement about serious leisure, which at the time, depicted its casual counterpart as all activity not classifiable as serious (project-based leisure has since been added as a third form, see next section). As a scientific concept, casual leisure languished in this residual status, until Stebbins (1997a; 2001c), belatedly recognizing its centrality and importance in leisure studies, sought to elaborate the idea as a sensitizing concept for exploratory research, as he had earlier for serious leisure (see also Rojek, 1997). It is considerably less substantial and offers no career of the sort found in serious leisure.

Its types – there are eight—include *play* (including dabbling), relaxation (e.g., sitting, napping, strolling), *passive entertainment* (e.g., TV, books, recorded music), *active entertainment* (e.g., games of chance, party games), *sociable conversation*, *sensory stimulation* (e.g., sex, eating, drinking), and *casual volunteering* (as opposed to serious leisure, or career, volunteering). Note that dabbling (as play) may occur in the same genre of activity pursued by amateurs, hobbyists, and career volunteers. The preceding section was designed, in part, to conceptually separate dabblers from this trio of leisure participants, thereby enabling the reader to interpret with sophistication references to, for example, "amateurish" activity (e.g., *The Cult of the Amateur,* by Keen, 2007)

The last and newest type of casual leisure – *pleasurable aerobic activity* – refers to physical activities that require effort sufficient to cause marked increase in respiration and heart rate. Here I am referring to "aerobic activity" in the broad sense, to all activity that calls for such effort, which to be sure, includes the routines pursued collectively in (narrowly conceived of) aerobics classes and those pursued individually by way of televised or video-taped programs of aerobics (Stebbins, 2004b). Yet, as with its passive and active cousins in entertainment, pleasurable aerobic activity is basically casual leisure. That is, to do such activity requires little more than minimal skill, knowledge, or experience. Examples include the game of the Hash House Harriers (a type of treasure hunt in the outdoors), kickball (described in the *Economist*, 2005, as a cross between soccer and baseball), and such children's games as hide-and-seek.

It is likely that people pursue the different types of casual leisure in combinations of two and three at least as often as they pursue them separately. For instance, every type can be relaxing, producing in this fashion play-relaxation, passive entertainment-relaxation, and so on. Various combinations of play and sensory stimulation are also possible, as in experimenting, in deviant or non-deviant ways, with drug use, sexual activity, and thrill seeking through movement. Additionally, sociable conversation accompanies some sessions of sensory stimulation (e.g., recreational drug use, curiosity seeking, displays of beauty) as well as some sessions of relaxation and active and passive entertainment, although such conversation normally tends to be rather truncated in the latter two.

Notwithstanding its hedonic nature casual leisure is by no means wholly inconsequential, for some clear costs and benefits accrue from pursuing it. Moreover, in contrast to the evanescent hedonic property of casual leisure itself, these costs and benefits are enduring. The benefits include serendipitous creativity and discovery in play, regeneration from early intense activity, and development and maintenance of interpersonal relationships (Stebbins, 2001c; other benefits are discussed in Stebbins, 2006, pp. 41-43). Some of its costs root in excessive casual leisure or lack of variety as manifested in boredom or lack of time for leisure activities that contribute to self through acquisition of skills, knowledge, and experience (i.e., serious leisure). Moreover, casual leisure is alone unlikely to produce a distinctive leisure identity.

Project-Based Leisure

Project-based leisure (Stebbins, 2005c) is the third form of leisure activity and the most recent one added to the Perspective. It is a short-term, reasonably complicated, one-off or occasional, though infrequent, creative undertaking carried out in free time, or time free of disagreeable obligation. Such leisure requires considerable planning, effort, and sometimes skill or knowledge, but is, for all that, neither serious leisure nor intended to develop into such. Examples include surprise birthday parties, elaborate preparations for a major holiday, and volunteering for sports events. Though only a rudimentary social world springs up around the project, it does, in its own particular way, bring together friends, neighbors, or relatives (e.g., through a genealogical project or Christmas celebrations), or draw the individual participant into an organizational milieu (e.g., through volunteering for a sports event or major convention).

Types of Project-Based Leisure

It was noted in the definition just presented that project-based leisure is not all the same. Whereas systematic exploration may reveal others, two types are evident at this time: one-shot projects and occasional projects. These are presented next using an earlier classificatory framework for amateur, hobbyist, and volunteer activities developed by the author (see Stebbins, 1998a, chaps. 2-4).

One-Shot Projects

In all these projects people generally use the talents and knowledge they have at hand, even though for some projects they may seek certain instructions beforehand, including reading a book or taking a short course. And some projects resembling hobbyist activity participation may require a modicum of preliminary conditioning. Always, the goal is to undertake successfully the one-shot project and nothing more, and sometimes a small amount of background preparation is necessary for this. It is possible that a survey would show that most project-based leisure is hobbyist in character and the next most common, a kind of volunteering. First, the following hobbyist-like projects have so far been identified:

- Making and tinkering:
  - o Interlacing, interlocking, and knot-making from kits
  - o Other kit assembly projects (e.g., stereo tuner, craft store projects)
  - o Do-it-yourself projects done primarily for fulfillment, some of which may even be undertaken with minimal skill and knowledge (e.g., build a rock wall or a fence, finish a room in the basement, plant a special garden). This could turn into an irregular series of such projects, spread over many years, possibly even transforming the participant into a hobbyist.
- Liberal arts:
  - o Genealogy (not as ongoing hobby)
  - o Tourism: special trip, not as part of an extensive personal tour program, to visit different parts of a region, a continent, or much of the world
- Activity participation: long back-packing trip, canoe trip; one-shot mountain ascent (e.g., Fuji, Rainier, Kilimanjaro)

One-shot volunteering projects are also common, though possibly somewhat less so than hobbyist-like projects. And less common than either are the amateur-like projects, which seem to concentrate in the sphere of theater.

- Volunteering
  - o   Volunteer at a convention or conference, whether local, national, or international in scope.
  - o   Volunteer at a sporting competition, whether local, national, or international in scope.
  - o   Volunteer at an arts festival or special exhibition mounted in a museum.
  - o   Volunteer to help restore human life or wildlife after a natural or human-made disaster caused by, for instance, a hurricane, earthquake, oil spill, or industrial accident.
- Entertainment Theater: produce a skit (a form of sketch) or one-shot community pageant; create a puppet show; prepare a home film or a set of videos, slides, or photos; prepare a public talk.

Occasional Projects

The occasional projects seem more likely to originate in or be motivated by agreeable obligation than their one-shot cousins. Examples of occasional projects include the sum of the culinary, decorative, or other creative activities undertaken, for example, at home or at work for a religious occasion or someone's birthday. Likewise, national holidays and similar celebrations sometimes inspire individuals to mount occasional projects consisting of an ensemble of inventive elements.

Unlike one-shot projects occasional projects have the potential to become routinized, which happens when new creative possibilities no longer come to mind as the participant arrives at a fulfilling formula wanting no further modification. North Americans who decorate their homes the same way each Christmas season exemplify this situation. Indeed, it can happen that, over the years, such projects may lose their appeal, but not their necessity, thereby becoming disagreeable obligations, which their authors no longer define as leisure.

And, lest it be overlooked, note that one-shot projects also hold the possibility of becoming unpleasant. Thus, the hobbyist genealogist gets overwhelmed with the details of family history and the difficulty of verifying dates. The thought of putting in time and effort doing something once considered leisure but which she now dislikes makes no sense. Likewise, volunteering for a project may turn sour, creating in the volunteer a sense of being faced with a disagreeable obligation, which however, must still be honored. This is leisure no more.

Work

Work, says Applebaum (1992, p. x), has no satisfactory definition, since the idea relates to all human activities. That caveat aside, he sees work, among other ways, as performance of useful activity (making things, performing services) done as all or part of sustaining life, as a livelihood. Some people are remunerated for their work, whereas others get paid in kind or directly keep body and soul together with the fruits of their labor (e.g., subsistence farming, hunting, fishing). Work, thus defined, is as old as humankind, since all save a few privileged people have always had to seek a livelihood. The same may be said for leisure, to the extent that some free time has always existed after work. Today, in the West, most work of the kind considered here is remunerated, but the non-remunerated variety is evident, too. The most celebrated example of the latter is house work, but there are also livelihood activities that we tend to define as non-work obligation (e.g., do-it-yourself house repairs, money-saving dress making). Work, as just defined, is activity people have to do, if they are to meet their economic needs. And, though some exceptions are examined later in this section, most people do not particularly like their work. If, for example, their livelihood were somehow guaranteed, they would take up more pleasant activities, assuming of course, they are aware of them.

For many Westerners working time is a major part of everyday life, commonly eating up many hours a week from age seventeen or eighteen to sixty-five or seventy, and nowadays, even older. So work is not only this person's livelihood, it is also a major component of his or her lifestyle. But to keep work in perspective, we need to underscore further how much of life for the Westerner is actually not work at all, in that it consists of activity other than that devoted to making a living. In this regard, Applebaum's definition overlooks the fact that making things and performing services can also occur as serious leisure, as any furniture maker or volunteer, for example, would happily acknowledge.

Moreover, work is not even a universal feature of most Westerners' life long existence. First, during childhood and adolescence, most people are not engaged, or are engaged rather little, in work activities. Second, during their working years, some people wind up being unemployed (get fired, laid off, disabled), placing them at least temporarily outside the work force. Third, most people retire, though this status is fuzzy because some of them remain partially employed during some or all of this stage of life.

Fourth, even when working full-time in the West as measured by a nation's average work week, workers typically have considerably more free time than work time. That is we all exist in a week of 168 hours. Let us estimate that, on average, seventy of those hours go for sleep and bodily maintenance (including fitness activity) taken after a modern thirty-six-hour average workweek. According to this formula sixty-two hours remain for family, leisure, and non-work obligations. The *Economist* (2006) reports that the time working-age Americans, for example, devote to leisure activities has risen by four to eight hours a week over the past four decades. This pattern is broken by those who decide (or are forced) to work longer hours or are pressed to put in excessive time meeting non-work obligations.

What is critical for positive sociology in all this is the presence of a small proportion of the working population in the West who find it difficult to separate their work and leisure. These workers, for whom the line between the two domains is blurred, do rely on their work as a livelihood, but nevertheless are also "occupational devotees" (Stebbins, 2004a).[5] That is they feel a powerful *occupational devotion*, or strong, positive attachment to a form of self-enhancing work, where the sense of achievement is high and the core activity is endowed with such intense appeal that the line between this work and leisure is virtually erased. Further, it is by way of the core activity of their work devotees realize a unique combination of, what are for them, strongly seated cultural values (Williams, 2000, p. 146): success, achievement, freedom of action, individual personality, and activity (being involved in something). Other categories of workers may also be animated by some, even all, of these values, but fail for various reasons to realize them in gainful employment.

Occupational devotees turn up chiefly, though not exclusively, in four areas of the economy, providing their work there is, at most, only lightly bureaucratized: certain small businesses, the skilled trades, the consulting and counseling occupations, and the public- and client-centered professions. Public-centered professions are found in the arts, sports, scientific, and entertainment fields, while those that are client-centered abound in such fields as law, teaching, accounting, and medicine (Stebbins, 1992, p. 22). It is assumed in all this that the work and its core activity to which people become devoted carries with it a respectable personal and social identity within their reference groups, since it would be difficult, if not impossible, to be devoted to work that those groups regarded with scorn. Still, positive identification with the job is not a defining condition of occupational devotion, since such identification can develop for other reasons, including high salary, prestigious employer, and advanced educational qualifications.

The fact of devotee work for some people and its possibility for others signals that work, as one of life's domains, may be positive. Granted, most workers are not fortunate enough to find such work. For those who do find it, the work meets six criteria (Stebbins, 2004a, p. 9). To generate occupational devotion:

1. The valued core activity must be profound; to perform it acceptability requires substantial skill, knowledge, or experience or a combination of two or three of these.
2. The core must offer significant variety.
3. The core must also offer significant opportunity for creative or innovative work, as a valued expression of individual personality. The adjectives "creative" and "innovative" stress that the undertaking results in something new or different, showing imagination and application of routine skill or knowledge. That is, boredom is likely to develop only after the onset of fatigue experienced from long hours on the job, a point at which significant creativity and innovation are no longer possible.
4. The would-be devotee must have reasonable control over the amount and disposition of time put into the occupation (the value of freedom of action), such that he can prevent it from becoming a burden. Medium and large bureaucracies have tended to subvert this criterion. For, in interest of the survival and development of their organization, managers have felt they must deny their nonunionized employees this freedom, and force them to accept stiff deadlines and heavy workloads. But no activity, be it leisure or work, is so appealing that it invites unlimited participation during all waking hours.
5. The would-be devotee must have both an aptitude and a taste for the work in question. This is, in part, a case of one man's meat being another man's poison. John finds great fulfillment in being a physician, an occupation that holds little appeal for Jane who, instead, adores being a lawyer (work John finds unappealing).
6. The devotees must work in a physical and social milieu that encourages them to pursue often and without significant constraint the core activity. This includes avoidance of excessive paperwork, caseloads, class sizes, market demands, and the like.

Sounds ideal, if not idealistic, but in fact occupations and work roles exist that meet these criteria. These criteria also characterize serious leisure (see Stebbins, 2004a, chap. 4), which gives further substance to the claim being put forward here that such leisure and devotee work occupy a great deal of common ground. When this happens the scope of positive sociology extends beyond the domain of leisure into that of work.

Non-Work Obligation

Obligation outside that experienced while pursuing a livelihood is terribly understudied (much of it falls under the heading of family and/or domestic life, while obligatory communal involvements are also possible) and sometimes seriously misunderstood (as in coerced "volunteering"). To speak of obligation, is to speak not about how people are prevented from entering certain leisure activities—the object of much of research on leisure constraints—but about how people fail to define a given activity as leisure or redefine it as other than leisure, as an unpleasant obligation. Obligation is both a state of mind, an attitude – a person feels obligated—and a form of behavior—he must carry out a particular course of action, engage in a particular activity. But even while obligation is substantially mental and behavioral, it roots, too, in the social and cultural world of the obligated actor. Consequently, we may even speak of a culture of obligation that takes shape around many work, leisure, and non-work activities (to be discussed further in chap. 3).

Obligation fits with positive sociology in at least two ways: leisure may include certain agreeable obligations and the third domain of life – non-work obligation – consists of disagreeable requirements capable of undermining positiveness. *Agreeable obligation* is very much a part of some leisure, evident when such obligation accompanies positive commitment to an activity that evokes pleasant memories and expectations (these two are essential features of leisure, Kaplan, 1960, pp. 22-25). Still, it might be argued that agreeable obligation in leisure is not really felt as obligation, since the participant wants to do the activity anyway. But my research in serious leisure suggests a more complicated picture. My respondents knew that they were supposed to be at a certain place or do a certain thing and knew that they had to make this a priority in their day-to-day living (this exemplifies discretionary time commitment, chap. 3). They not only wanted to do this, they were also required to do it; other activities and demands could wait. At times, the participant's intimates objected to the way he or she prioritized everyday commitments, and this led to friction, creating costs for the first that somewhat diluted the rewards of the leisure in question. Agreeable obligation is also found in devotee work and the other two forms of leisure, though possibly least so in casual leisure.

On the other hand *disagreeable obligation* has no place in leisure, because, among other reasons, it fails to leave the participant with a pleasant memory or expectation of the activity. Rather it is the stuff of the third domain: non-work obligation. This domain is the classificatory home of all we must do that we would rather avoid that is not related to work (including moonlighting). So far I have been able to identify three types.

Unpaid labor: activities people do themselves even though services exist which they could hire to carry them out. These activities include mowing the lawn, house work, shoveling the sidewalk, preparing the annual income tax return, do-it-yourself, and a myriad of obligations to friends and family (e.g., caring for a sick relative, helping a friend move to another home, arranging a funeral).

Unpleasant tasks: required activities for which no commercial services exist or, if they exist, most people would avoid using them. Such activities are exemplified in checking in and clearing security at airports, attending a meeting on a community problem, walking the dog each day, driving in city traffic (in this discussion, beyond that related to work), and errands, including routine grocery shopping. There are also obligations to family and friends in this type, among them, driving a child to soccer practice and mediating familial quarrels. Many of the "chores" of childhood fall in this category. Finally, activities sometimes mislabelled as volunteering are, in fact, disagreeable obligations from which the individual senses no escape. For example some parents feel this way about coaching their children's sports teams or about helping out with a road trip for the youth orchestra in which their children play.

Self-care: disagreeable activities designed to maintain or improve in some way the physical or psychological state of the individual. They include getting a hair cut, putting on cosmetics, doing health-promoting exercises, going to the dentist, and undergoing a physical examination. Personal and family counselling also fall within this type, as do the activities that accompany getting a divorce.

Some activities in these types are routine obligations, whereas others are only occasional. And, for those who find some significant measure of enjoyment in, say, grocery shopping, walking the dog, do-it-yourself, or taking physical exercise, these obligations are defined as agreeable; they are effectively leisure. Thus what is disagreeable in the domain of non-work obligation rests on personal interpretation of the actual or anticipated experience of an activity. So most people dislike or expect to dislike their annual physical examination, but not the hypochondriac.

Non-work obligation, even if it tends to occupy less time than the other two domains, is not therefore inconsequential. I believe the foregoing types support this observation. Moreover some of them may be gendered (e.g., housework), and accordingly, occasional sources of friction and attenuated positiveness of lifestyle for all concerned. Another leading concern for positive sociology laid down by non-work obligation is that the second reduces further (after work is done) the amount of free time for leisure and, for some people, devotee work. Such obligation may threaten the latter, because it may reduce the time occupational devotees who, enamored as they are of their core work activities, would like to put in at work, as in effect, overtime.

Conclusion

Positive sociology looks on this discussion of non-work obligation and, to some extent, occupational obligation as, in part, a matter of use of time. How much time must we devote to work and to the unpleasant activities required of us outside that domain? There is, in principle, for each person, a degree of flexibility in responding this question. That is, how much work do we judge to be enough for a livelihood? How many obligated non-work activities are absolutely necessary, which could be re-evaluated as not obligatory?

This, many readers will recognize, is the essence of the contemporary issue known as "work/life" balance. Much of this book revolves around it, with the issue being considered most deeply in chapters 3 and 7. Still, from what has been said so far, non-work obligation might seem to be a weak or insignificant domain vis-à-vis those of work and leisure. For instance, compared with the other two, it was covered in the fewest number of pages in the present chapter. Furthermore some of the examples in that section may appear trivial, whereas as others may seem to be profound and absolutely inescapable. Nevertheless I hope to show in the course of this book that the domain of non-work obligation is a sort of wild card in the game of life; if played properly it can help us succeed in establishing one of two special lifestyles: optimal leisure lifestyle and optimal positive lifestyle. In turn it is precisely these lifestyles that form the basis for the kind of world that a positive sociology can both study and foster.

These two lifestyles will be formally introduced in chapter 3, and then carried on through the book as leitmotifs. Before this, however, some historical background of the three domains is in order.

Notes

1.   Parts of sociology are neither positive nor negative, as these terms are used here. The discipline, especially in its early years, has also been given to describing in

neutral language such phenomena as social organization, demographic patterns, and group culture.

2.   I am aware that standard sociological theory conceives of roles as dynamic and statuses as static. Compared with activities, however, roles are *relatively* static.

3.   The serious leisure perspective and its three forms are discussed in considerably greater detail in Stebbins (1992; 2001a; and 2006).

4.   We return to the subject of values in chapter 6 and a discussion of cultural values and their relationship to the personal reward-values considered in the present chapter.

5.   For a discussion from a different angle of workers who are devoted to their work, see Gini (2001, p. 15 et passim).

2

A History of Work, Leisure, and Obligation

"No man is born into the world whose work is not born with him: there is always work, And tools to work withal, for those who will; And blessed are the horny hand of toil!"—James Russell Lowell, A Glance Behind the Curtain (l. 202)

According to Duval (2003, p. 17) leisure and work are cultural universals; all societies in all periods of history have exhibited a continuum of use of time linking these two. The object of this chapter is, first, to show, albeit in general terms, the validity of this observation and, then, set out in somewhat greater detail the modern place of work, leisure, and obligation. The intention is to create a sense of where these three domains have recently come from so as to understand better where they may be headed in the future.

Subsistence Societies

Viewed from the standpoint of work and leisure, much of the history of mankind has been about subsistence as a livelihood, with free-time activity taking place in the comparatively few hours left over after seeing to life's basic needs. Hunting, fishing, and gathering food; raising and harvesting crops; and moving to new land that facilitates all of these, along with defending against enemies, human and animal, occupy a lot of time in a preindustrial society. But life on this subsistence level must necessarily include a few hours off for games, dancing, music, relaxation, sexual activity, casual conversation, and the like.

Hamilton-Smith (2003, pp. 225-226) writes that archaeological findings on this sort of leisure gathered from artifacts, living sites, cave painting, and so on dates as far back as the prehistoric cultures. McBrearty and Stringer (2007) write that

> all humans today express their social status and group identity through visual clues such as clothing, jewelry, cosmetics and hairstyle. Shell beads, and haematite used

> as pigment, show that this behaviour dates to 80,000 years ago in coastal North and South Africa.... Ochre seems to have been a material with both symbolic and utilitarian functions. The colour red is fundamental to colour classifications in all known human societies, and it seems probable that the substance was indeed used for body painting and to colour artefacts by 165,000 years ago. (764)

Since there seems to be no evidence on the matter, we may only speculate that some disagreeable non-work obligations also troubled subsistence peoples, whatever the time in history during which they lived. Some of these may have been religious, exemplified in carrying out animal and human sacrifices and participating in sacred rituals. Perhaps there was also the occasional need for mediating family differences, in addition to engaging in activities intended to uphold honor and mete out justice to those felt to have violated group rules. Further it is conceivable that, in their own way, these societies ministered to their sick and injured, arranging for customary disposal of the dead when these actions failed.

In this discussion of work, leisure, and obligation in subsistence times, I have used these concepts as defined in the preceding chapter. Still it is doubtful that people living then were oriented by these ideas. Nevertheless they did believe in what they had to do to survive in their world, however scientifically accurate this knowledge. Furthermore the activities implementing the knowledge were not seen as optional. Today we call this work. Additionally there were activities that would seem to be optional as well as enjoyable, including relaxing, dancing, making and listening to music, and at least some of the time, sexual relations. In modern times this is leisure. But what about obligations? I suspect that, though they must have existed then, they were probably poorly understood, or understood simply as customary activities people are supposed to engage in. In this regard little has changed, for the modern commonsense understanding of the idea is, at bottom, only marginally more advanced.

Furthermore, work and leisure, however understood, were probably in these societies also sometimes difficult to distinguish. If the hunt is a fulfilling work activity (consisting of, for instance, skill in tracking, knowledge of animal habits, developed prowess with bow or spear), whatever the basic need it fills, is it not akin to the occupational devotion of the modern age? Is not decorating a clay pot, which with this activity pushes it beyond its utilitarian value as a receptacle for water, also an expression of an acquired artistic skill? Again, does this not resemble devotee work? In short, occupational devotion may be far older than suggested in the preceding chapter.

Western Societies

Sylvester (1999, pp. 18-23) writes that, from classical antiquity through the Middle Ages, two streams of thought influenced modern-day Western beliefs about and attitudes toward work and leisure. One had its roots in ancient Greece, especially in the city-state of Athens, while the other emerged later in the ferment of early Christianity.

Classical Greece[1]

The actual patterns of work and leisure among ordinary people during this period, it appears, were quite different from what its "gentlemen-philosophers" – most notably Plato and Aristotle – had to say about them (Sylvester, 1999, p. 18). These intellectuals were unusual people in Greek society, for they had sufficient free time during which they could philosophize about these two domains and their relationship. We will concentrate in this section on some of the key ideas of the two men, primarily because those ideas have had considerable impact on Western thought on work and leisure and because the historical record of these domains in the rest of ancient Greek society is inadequate.

Plato argued that leisure was a necessary condition for anyone devoting himself to the activity of discovering truth (use of masculine gender is intentional here, for females were not considered part of this class). The thinker engaged in this pursuit had to be free from the demands of securing a livelihood. As for the discovery of truth, this was strictly the province of intellectuals of superior breeding. In particular, these intellectuals were philosophers; they were the only people capable of discovering truth, or "knowledge," while also providing civic leadership. The truth in question, by the way, was not knowledge based on sensory experience (sight, taste, touch, etc.), subject to change in light of new empirical evidence – scientific knowledge—but rather knowledge in the unchangeable, transcendental shape of ideas, or "forms" – philosophical knowledge.

In this system, the common man, who was sometimes a slave, labored for his own livelihood as well as that of the gentlemen-philosophers. Such was his lot in life. Work is honored here because it supports someone else's freedom from work and that person's pursuit of excellence in the creation of knowledge. Of course, the ordinary worker gained little more from all this than his livelihood.

Aristotle wrote about what has been translated into English as the "good life." Integral to this life, he said, is achieving excellence in morality and intellectual pursuits. Moral excellence, he argued, comes with contemplating how best to live both individually and socially, whereas intellectual excellence grows from understanding and delighting in the true principles of the universe. Also included in the good life is engaging in such activities as speech (oratory), music, friendship, gymnastics, and citizenship. Moreover, according to Sylvester (1999, p. 20), Aristotle viewed work as "severely encroaching on the good life. Only when people were liberated from having to work for the necessities of life could they turn to the good life." It follows that leisure, which in ancient Greece was freedom from having to work, is itself a condition of the good life. Consistent with this line of reasoning was Aristotle's assertion that happiness also depends on leisure.

A citizen, or a person holding citizenship in a Greek city-state, also enjoyed leisure. Yet, as such, he was no laborer. Furthermore, citizens were expected to keep themselves geographically apart from the rest, from noncitizens. The former even had their special agora, in which leisure on the order of the activities listed in the preceding paragraph was pursued. By contrast the agora of the latter was a place for trade, a commercial arena for facilitating the exchange of things the working class made or grew.

Notwithstanding their self-serving model of society, neither Plato nor Aristotle viewed work as inherently demeaning. Rather, what was demeaning was the requirement that a person labor, for this created a dependence on work. In other words, if ordinary people fail to work, they will gain no livelihood and therefore soon perish. Additionally, the two philosophers maintained it is demeaning to be unable to experience happiness and realize excellence, both being achievable only during leisure.

Sylvester (1999, pp. 21-23) qualifies the foregoing as an elitist conception of work and leisure in ancient Greece, noting further that, unfortunately, it is the only recorded statement on leisure available for that era. He explained that "by applying higher and more rigorous standards to the concept of freedom, aristocrats were able to underscore their superiority while defining the *demos* [common people] as unfree, licentious, and unworthy. Furthermore, aristocrats identified *freedom* from labor, a condition synonymous with leisure, as a vital form of freedom" (p. 22). As the aristocrats viewed the world the narrow training of the craftsman rendered him unfit for leisure. By contrast aristocratic training consisted of education in the liberal arts of music, philosophy, speech, and the like. Aristocratic excellence was further expressed in war, sport, and competitions in music, among other pursuits, all of which could be defined today as serious leisure.

Nonetheless, what little evidence there is suggests that the *demos* clearly took pride in their craftwork. But it also appears that they failed to value work for its own sake; as a general activity it was never glorified. In the language of this book, the *demos*, when its workers could find self-fulfillment in their labor, did certainly value its core activities and the products they created through their efforts. These craftsmen were independent workers, much like, we might say, some of the small-business crafts people of today, described earlier as occupational devotees.

The Judeo-Christian Era

During the Judeo-Christian period work came to be glorified, particularly as an avenue leading to spiritual development. Besides its necessity as a livelihood, work was thought to foster desirable habits, among them, sobriety, discipline, and industry. Furthermore, work engendered a certain independence in the worker and, apparently (Sylvester, 1999, p. 24), a sense of charity. Unlike in the days of ancient Greece, work in the Judeo-Christian tradition was ultimately held to be undertaken for the glory of God as well as to instill a level of sacredness in those who worked here on Earth.

In the Middle Ages, Christian monasticism revolved around work, through which the monks in retreat in monasteries sought religious purity in manual labor and the reading of divine literature. Leisure, in this situation, was held in low regard. It took St. Thomas Aquinas to restore it to the dignified position it enjoyed in ancient Greece. Aquinas argued that, if a man could live without labor, he was under no obligation to engage in it. Indeed spiritual work was only possible when the thinker was freed of physical labor. The elevated place of the contemplative life was thus restored, and with it the value of leisure.

With the advent of the Renaissance the balance of prestige between work and leisure shifted somewhat. This was a period of creative activity, which rested substantially on practical achievements in art and craft. Experimental physical science also took root during this era, initially as a (serious) leisure pursuit. Nevertheless the skilled artist, craftsman, and scientist were, themselves, special people. Ordinary manual laborers were still regarded as lowly by this group and the rest of the elite, thereby enabling these higher ranks in society to retain their superiority, backed by leisure as one of the differentiating principles.

The Protestant Reformation

Al Gini (2001, pp. 20-21) has observed that, together, the Renaissance and the Protestant Reformation have served as a cardinal reference point in the development of the modern work ethic. He points out that "it was during this period that work, no matter how high or low the actual task, began to develop a positive ethos of its own, at least at the theoretical level" (p. 20). More particularly, Sylvester (1999, p. 26) writes: "the Protestant work ethic was one of the central intellectual developments in changing attitudes toward labor and leisure. In it work is more than a livelihood, it is also a man's *raison d'être.*"

The Protestant ethic, seldom mentioned today in lay circles and possibly not much discussed there even during its highest point in the seventeenth and eighteenth centuries, has nevertheless been a prominent social force in the evolution of Western society. Culturally and structurally, this powerful personal orientation motivating the small-enterprise capitalists of the day left its mark, one so powerful that it is still being felt in the present. This is because the Protestant ethic is, at bottom, about the will to work.

Max Weber and the Protestant Ethic

Max Weber published, in German in 1904, the first section of his essay "The Protestant Ethic and the Spirit of Capitalism," shortly before he set out to visit the United States. Upon returning at the end of 1904 to his native Germany, he published (in 1905) the second part, which was much informed by his observations on American society and its capitalist economic system. Following Weber's death in 1920, the essay was reprinted, along with a number of lengthier works, in one of several large volumes released in the early 1920s. Not long thereafter, Talcott Parsons translated and published as a small book, with direct translation of the title, the only English edition of "The Protestant Ethic" (Weber, 1930).

Gerth and Mills (1958, p. 25) said of Weber that "although he was personally irreligious – in his own words, 'religiously unmusical' – he nevertheless spent a good part of his scholarly energy in tracing the effects of religion upon human conduct and life." Weber's treatise on the Protestant ethic and the spirit of capitalism – his most celebrated essay—is, among other things, about individual men (women are never mentioned in the essay) becoming motivated to pursue the value of success and achievement in an occupation defined by each as a divine calling. It is also about how Western capitalism as an economic system (as opposed to great individual undertakings) evolved in part from the activities of these men. Weber was interested in the worldly asceticism of seventeenth- and eighteenth-century Protestantism, of which Calvinism was the purest instance. In particular he was concerned with Calvin's principle of predestination. Calvin had argued that only a small proportion of all people are chosen for grace, or eternal salvation, whereas the rest are not. This arrangement cannot be changed, for it is God's will.

But, alas, the chosen do not know they have been chosen. The tension of not knowing whether you number among the elect could nevertheless be assuaged in this world by maintaining an implicit trust in Christ, the result of true faith. Moreover, it is a man's duty to consider himself chosen and to act as though this were true, evidence for which came from avoiding worldly temptations like sloth and the hedonic pleasures and from treating work as a calling. A calling—a task set by God but nonetheless chosen by mortals—refers as well to a man's duty to enact his occupational role to the best of his abilities, using his personal powers or material possessions and abstaining from creature pleasures and other leisure activities. This was measured, in part, by usefulness for the community of the goods produced in it. But the most important criterion was found in the realm of capitalist enterprise: amassing wealth through thrift, profit, diligence, investments, sobriety, and similar virtues, and not doing this as an end in-itself. Success and achievement in an occupation, whatever their nature, generate self-confidence, thereby reinforcing a man's belief that he has been chosen. In other words, God helps those who help themselves.

While acknowledging in passing that there were others, Weber concentrated primarily on "callings" or "professions" (referred to in this book in modern terms as "occupations") that made it possible to amass wealth. Achieving significant wealth helped generate self-confidence. Hard work, savings, investment, and shrewd decisions in commercial activities all constituted evidence of a man's belief in his own eternal salvation. The result was the emergence of a new social class of self-made entrepreneurs and soon thereafter their integration into the system of Western capitalism as we know it in the present. Weber's object of study was the men who established the family-firm type of capitalist business, common in Western Europe and the United States from the seventeenth century to the present.

According to Cohen (2002, p. 5) Weber was unclear about the relationship between modern capitalist institutions and the Puritans' spirit of capitalism. Still, from his extensive examination of historical evidence,

Cohen (2002, p. 254) was able to conclude that "English Puritanism aided capitalism, but its impact was weaker and less dramatic than Weber claimed." Moreover, the impact, attenuated as it was, was primarily cultural, in that helped legitimate further the emerging capitalism of the day and helped mold the broader work ethic as it was taking shape at that time in Occidental culture.

The Protestant Ethic Today

The Protestant ethic, as a summary concept for a distinctive set of motives to work, is largely a dead letter today (it was already in serious decline even at the time Weber wrote about it), though some people still work long hours in pursuit of a variety of more worldly rewards. David Riesman and colleagues (1961) argued that the inner-directed men of the 1950s, who *were* oriented by the Protestant ethic, were being rapidly replaced by other-directed men whose love of mass culture was their singular trait. Otherworldly in orientation as it was, the Protestant ethic, it appears, was nevertheless an important cultural precursor of the modern work ethic. It helped steer the search for the cultural value of activity toward the domain of work (as opposed to that of leisure); work is good and hard work is still better.

Although the Protestant ethic was, in fact, both a cultural and an individual phenomenon, Weber wrote mostly about its psychological side; he looked on the ascetic Protestants as constituting a distinctive type of personality with its own worldview. Analysis of the Protestant ethic as a personal worldview reveals three central components. One is attitude: a person should work, work hard, and avoid leisure as much as possible. The second is value: work activity is good, whereas leisure activity is not. The third component is belief: by hard work people can demonstrate their faith that they number among the chosen. On the macroanalytic level, we find in societies where the Protestant ethic is widely shared that all three personal components are also widely shared. Thus the Protestant ethic is also part of the culture of these societies. And speaking of culture, the Protestant ethic, as mentioned already, also contributed significantly to the rise of the economic system that came to be known as capitalism. That system is now a main social institution in modern Western society.

Another reason for the decline of the Protestant ethic is that it never could become the guiding orientation for all paid work, including certain kinds that were carried out even during the heyday of the ethic (Stebbins, 2004b, pp. 26-27). True, Weber wrote, albeit briefly, about all callings and the requirement that those pursuing them demonstrate through hard work their chosen place in Heaven. But then he went on to concentrate exclusively on the capitalist trades and the accumulation of wealth in that sphere. Perhaps, for Weber, the problem was that many other occupations fail to produce evidence of diligence so tangible, countable, and incontrovertible as property and monetary riches. As a result, in Weber's day, as in modern times, there were and still are numerous occupations that, at bottom, lie outside the purview of his essay, including those requiring altruistic service to humankind (e.g., nursing, teaching) and extensive development of personal skills and knowledge (e.g., science, sports, the arts).

It is quite possible therefore that, at the time when the Protestant ethic was a prominent motive for many workers, others were enamored instead of occupations with great intrinsic appeal, but which could offer as evidence of having been chosen few convincing ways of publicly displaying diligence and excellence. Put otherwise, these latter occupations were intrinsically attractive, a quality found in the enactment of the work itself rather than in extrinsic rewards it produced such as high remuneration and great profit. It was, in general, difficult to measure, simply and publicly, intrinsic rewards, such that they could constitute proof of the worker's place among the elect. In brief, occupational devotion lay beyond the scope of Weber's essay.

These intrinsically fulfilling occupations, which were in effect beyond the purview of the Protestant ethic, grew in importance during the twentieth century. And the modern "work ethic," being broader than its religious cousin, the Protestant ethic, finds expression in them as well. What, then, is the work ethic, the ethic that dominates in modern times?

The Work Ethic and Its Variants

By mid-twentieth century, the salvation component of the Protestant ethic can be observed, as already noted, only in the outlook of David Riesman's (Riesman et al, 1961) inner-directed man, who by then, was nevertheless a vanishing breed. What was left by that point in history of the West's distinctive orientation toward work has been known all along simply as the "work ethic." This more diffuse ethic, in fact, shares two of the three components of the Protestant version, mentioned earlier. It shares the same attitudes: a person should work, work hard, and avoid leisure as much as possible. It also shares the same values: work is good, while leisure is not. Only the third component is missing – that of belief: by hard work people can demonstrate their faith that they number among the chosen. In short, the work ethic is but a secular version of the Protestant ethic.

One widely discussed characteristic of today's work ethic has been described as "workaholism," an orientation that has probably been around as long as the work ethic itself and that may be seen as another offshoot of the Protestant ethic. Marilyn Machlowitz (1980) pioneered this concept, in an attempt to help explain why a conspicuous minority of modern workers, though not guided by the Protestant ethic, are still exceptionally drawn to their work. Part of this attraction is positive, she said; they find in their work many intrinsic rewards. The other part, however, is negative; that is they are also "work junkies," unfortunates lamentably addicted to their work. These people find joy and fulfillment in their work roles, from which they nonetheless seem compulsively unable to take any real holiday.

The positive, non-addictive side of workaholism bears a strong resemblance to occupational devotion. Thus the modern work ethic – most generally put that hard work is good – is manifested in at least two main ways among other ways: workaholism and occupational devotion. Generally speaking, the scope of the latter has shrunk in some ways. It has been buffeted by such forces as occupational deskilling and degradation (e.g., Braverman, 1974), industrial restructuring (e.g., downsizing), deindustrialization (e.g., plant closure and relocation), failed job improvement programs (e.g., the Human Relations and Quality of Work movements, Applebaum, 1992, p. 587), and overwork, whether required by employers or sought by workers craving extra income. Nevertheless, certain forms of devotion are more evident today than heretofore, seen for instance, in the rise of the independent consultant and the part-time professional.

But, alas, occupational devotion is a neologism, necessitated partly by the fact that workaholism, as a term, has through careless lay usage become corrupted and distorted to mean, now even for some scientists (e.g., Killinger, 1997; Sonnenberg, 1996), compulsion to work. Perhaps such distortion should have been expected, given that this sense of "ism" refers to the conduct of a class of people seen as much like that of another class, namely, people suffering from alcoholism. In this metaphorical stance compulsive workers, who toil well beyond providing for a reasonable lifestyle, are believed to find little of intrinsic worth in their work, instead they find only an irresistible impulse to engage in it. Workaholism will refer in this book only to this negative meaning, putting it thus beyond the scope of a positive sociology. These days most people speak most of the time about workaholics as work addicts, either forgetting or overlooking the fact that occupational devotees also exist.[2] Still some of those they casually label workaholic may well be devotees in both thought and action.

In the original, Machlowitzian version of the workaholism thesis, the passion people have for their work is explained, albeit in contradictory terms, by, in part, their love for it and by, in part, their addiction to it. Love suggests workers are attracted to their jobs by such rewards as self-fulfillment, self-expression, self-enrichment, and the like. These lead to deep occupational fulfillment. In contrast, addiction suggests workers are dragged to work by forces beyond their control. No rewards here of the sort just mentioned, rather there is only the compelling need to work and for many to make money, often in amounts well beyond those required for comfortable living. And, over the years, the term workaholism has come to mean exclusively this, with reference to a passion for work having rather quickly fallen into disfavor, perhaps because it so difficult these days to locate instances of it.

In sum, workaholism, occupational devotion, and the work ethic are, with some overlap in meaning, complementary orientations. The work ethic states that work is good, and it is important to do a good job while at it. Workaholism (adulterated version) states that, for some people, working is a compulsion. Occupational devotion includes the condition that work is intrinsically rewarding. The first and third are comprised of both attitudes and values, while the second seriously overextends the first, turning attitude and value into an uncontrollable drive to make money or simply do one's job, if not both. Combined, all three orientations constitute a substantial replacement of the Protestant ethic.

The Role of Leisure

Neither the Protestant ethic nor the work ethic accords a significant role to leisure. In this regard the first was particularly strict:

> The real moral objection is to relaxation in the security of possession, the enjoyment of wealth with the consequence of idleness and the temptations of the flesh, above all of distraction from the pursuit of a righteous life. In fact, it is only because possession involves this danger of relaxation that it is objectionable at all. For the saints' everlasting rest is in the next world; on earth man must, to be certain of his state of grace, "do the works of him who sent him, as long as it is yet day." Not leisure and enjoyment, but only activity serves to increase the glory of God, according to the definite manifestations of His will. (Weber, 1930, p. 157)

Waste of time, be it in sociability, idle talk, luxury, or excessive sleep, was considered the worst of all sins. Bluntly put, unwillingness to work was held as evidence of lack of grace. Sport received a partial reprieve from this fierce indictment, but only so far as it regenerated physical efficiency leading to improved productivity at work (Weber, 1930, p. 167).

By mid-nineteenth century in Europe and North America leisure had, with the weakening of the Protestant ethic, nonetheless gained a margin of respectability. Gelber (1999, p.1) observed that "industrialism quarantined work from leisure in a way that made employment more work-like and non-work more problematic. Isolated from each other's moderating influences, work and leisure became increasingly oppositional as they competed for finite hours." Americans, he said, responded in two ways to the threat posed by leisure as potential mischief caused by idle hands. Reformers tried to eliminate or at least restrict access to inappropriate activity, while encouraging people to seek socially approved free-time outlets. Hobbies and other serious leisure pursuits were high on the list of such outlets. In short, "the ideology of the workplace infiltrated the home in the form of productive leisure" (Gelber, 1999, p. 2).

Hobbies were particularly valued, because they bridged especially well the worlds of work and home. And both sexes found them appealing, albeit mostly not the same ones. Some hobbies allowed home-bound women to practice, and therefore understand, work-like activities, whereas other hobbies allowed men to create in the female-dominated house their own businesslike space – the shop in the basement or the garage. Among the various hobbies, two types stood out as almost universally approved in these terms: collecting and handicrafts. Still, before approximately 1880, before becoming defined as productive use of free time, these two, along with the other hobbies, were maligned as "dangerous obsessions."

Gelber (1999, pp. 3-4) notes that, although the forms of collecting and craftwork have changed somewhat during the past 150 years, their meaning has remained the same. Hobbies have, all along, been "a way to confirm the verities of work and the free market inside the home so long as remunerative employment has remained elsewhere" (p. 4).

If, in the later nineteenth century, the Protestant ethic was no longer a driving force for much of the working population, its surviving components in the work ethic were. Gary Cross (1990, chap. 7) concluded that, during much of this century, employers and upwardly mobile employees looked on "idleness" as threatening industrial development and social stability. The reformers in their midst sought to eliminate this "menace" by, among other approaches, attempting to build bridges to the "dangerous classes" in the new cities and, by this means, to transform them in the image of the middle class. This led to efforts to impose (largely rural) middle-class values on this group, while trying to instill a desire to engage in rational recreation—in modern terms, serious leisure—and consequently to seek less casual leisure.

But times have changed even more. Applebaum (1992, p. 587) writes that "with increases in the standard of living, consumerism, and leisure activities, the work ethic must compete with the ethic of the quality of life based on the release from work." And as the work ethic withers further in the twenty-first century, in the face of widespread reduction of work opportunities (e.g., Rifkin, 1995; Aronowitz & Difazio, 1994), leisure is slowly, but inexorably it appears, coming to the fore. In other words leisure has, since the middle nineteenth century, been evolving into an institution in its own right. At first leisure was a poor, underdeveloped institution, standing in pitiful contrast next to its robust counterpart of work. But now the twin ideas that work is inherently good and that, when it can be found, people should do it (instead of leisure) are now being increasingly challenged. Beck (2000, p. 125) glimpses the near future as a time when there will still work to be done, but of which a significant portion will be done without remuneration.

The counter-model to the work society is based not upon leisure but upon political freedom; it is a multi-activity society in which housework, family work, club work, and voluntary work are prized alongside paid work and returned to the center of public and academic attention. For in the end, these other forms remained trapped inside a value imperialism of work, which must be shaken off.

Beck calls this work without pay "civil labor." Some of it, however, especially club work and voluntary work, is also leisure, for it fits perfectly the definition of "serious leisure" set out in chapter 1: the intensely fulfilling free time activity of amateurs, hobbyists, and skilled and knowledgeable career volunteers.

Non-Work Obligation

Non-work obligation, being a new scientific concept (though, in the commonsense world, it is likely that many people have long recognized the phenomenon), a history of it remains to be written. In the present chapter, in the section on subsistence societies, I speculated about this domain but then dropped the subject after that. Nonetheless I am convinced that people have also faced a range of non-work obligations from the days of ancient Greece to the present, possibly many of them being similar to those described in the subsistence societies.

For the same reason it is no easier to find historical evidence on or analysis of non-work obligation in the past two to three centuries than before this period. To be sure, certain obligations have been considered, particularly in the present, in spheres where they are notoriously contentious, namely, housework, do-it-yourself, and parents' facilitation of the school and extracurricular activities of their children. But the academic literature in these areas has little to say about the history of such activities.

Even in do-it-yourself, where there is a modicum of historical literature, writing centers almost exclusively on the leisure facet of these activities (e.g., Gelber, 1999, chap. 10). Cross and Logemann (2004, p. 448) hint at the obligatory facet of do-it-self when, in commenting on its history, they observe that "the boundary between home improvement as work and leisure was certainly porous for most men of relatively modest means and without servants." Nevertheless their treatment of this subject is otherwise conducted from the angle of free-time activity.

The historical as well as contemporary social conditions framing conduct of our non-work obligatory activities are enormously important here. A few examples must suffice. Many a householder, past and present, has felt pressed to present a neat and clean residence to visitors, which is obligatory activity carried out to the tune of a cultural value emphasizing these two criteria. Or how many people in democratic societies vote in elections not because they see the activity of voting as leisure but because they feel it as a political, culturally based duty? And what about bureaucratic red tape and organizational rigidity as experienced when trying to claim an insured reimbursement for medical expenses, establish oneself as a candidate for political office (when defined as civic obligation), or introduce a change in regulations through the local school board or municipal government? In brief any proper history of non-work obligation will also need to address itself to the plethora and diversity of underlying social conditions in which these activities are pursued.

Conclusions

It has been illuminating to look on contemporary Western society from the standpoint of the Protestant ethic and its ramifications as felt over the years. First, this chapter has given historical depth to our understanding of the modern work ethic, at a time when it faces even greater challenges in the Information Age of the twenty-first century. Likewise, we have added such depth to our understanding of the role of leisure vis-à-vis that of work, accomplished in the main by charting the way leisure has been slowly but surely inching its way toward center stage, once exclusively the preserve of work. Except for the ancient philosophers, leisure has, down through modern history, been seen mostly as villain, for ever perturbing the hero of work. But the future augurs well for a more even balance in the importance of the two for some people and an imbalance skewed toward leisure for many others. In this new world those preferring work over leisure will, it appears, be but a small minority, composed mainly of two types: occupational devotees and stressed-out workaholics.

Second, this chapter reflects the extent to which we in the West have passed from a sacred to a secular society. For the vast majority of people here, work has little or nothing to do with the next world, unless of course, it is religious work. The social and psychological milieu of the ascetic Protestant, rooted as it was in small rural communities of an earlier era, was the antithesis of the sensual, increasingly leisure-oriented world of the urbanized worker of modern times.

Today, the Protestant ethic is, as I have argued, a dead letter. Occasionally, a person describes another as a hard worker imbued with this orientation, but such comments are becoming more infrequent with each passing year. Perhaps, too, the comments seem to come mostly from older people who still remember hearing about the Protestant ethic, even if, in their present-day application of it, they really have in mind nothing more than the broader, albeit simpler, idea of the work ethic. How many people today really think that a person's hard work springs from his desire to demonstrate his election in the hereafter? Be that as it may, the Protestant ethic was an important link in the chain of social conditions leading to the rise of Western capitalism and the framing of the work ethic as we now know both. On the whole, it appears that we are better off having passed through this phase of human social development, as protracted as it has been. And, to be sure, some people, Charles Darwin among them, have always managed to escape its clutches:

> [Being offered a job on the *Beagle*] was further evidence of his [Darwins's father] son's aimless preoccupation with enjoying himself. The voyage would be a useless, dangerous distraction. The unsettling years [five of them] in the company of sailors would taint Charles and spoil him for the Church. It would ruin his professional chances again. . . . The whole plan looked restless. (Desmond & Moore, 1991, p. 102)

In this conclusion I have taken, as I said I would, the Protestant ethic as a main turning point in the evolution of work and leisure in a time frame running from subsistence to modern living. Still we can hardly deny Plato and Aristotle's far-reaching influence on the contemporary world. Their speculations set the tone for the medieval debate on work vis-à-vis leisure, particularly as found in the thought of St. Thomas Aquinas. And the ascetic Protestantism of the reformation, of Calvin,

Luther, and others, flowed in significant measure from his words. The contemporary world of leisure is, understandably, quite different from that described by the two ancient philosophers. Yet, they were, in effect, discussing serious leisure for themselves, in one breath, while contrasting it with the casual leisure of the *demos*, in another. It is precisely along these lines that Aristotle is frequently quoted in today's leisure studies literature. Both Plato and Aristotle were convinced that the common man wastes too much time enjoying hedonic pleasure; in modern terms the *demos* were held to have had a warped view of how life's activities should be balancèd.

Notes

1.   This section and the next draw substantially on Charles Sylvester's (1999) excellent description and analysis of leisure, as philosophized in ancient Greek and early Judeo-Christian thought.
2.   Addictive workaholism is said to have become global. Moreover, take note, treatment for this affliction is now available in, among other forms, Workaholics Anonymous (Rushe, 2007).

3

Balancing Work, Leisure, and Obligation

> *"Canadians don't live to work, but work to live, according to a survey
> released Tuesday in anticipation of Mental Health Week, May 7-13.
> They say family, honesty and good health are far more important to
> them than work or money.*
> *And, while many are working longer and harder than ever, only one in
> five describe themselves as workaholics.*
> *However, 65 per cent feel that the values at their workplace are not in
> tune with their personal values and only one in four believe work-life
> balance is possible."—Kane, 2007*

The locution "work/leisure/obligation balance" describes better the
issue of finding a workable balance of activity in everyday life than its two
popular counterparts of "work/family balance" and "work/life balance."
The overall goal of this chapter is to explore why this tripartite balance
is important in the twenty-first century. We begin with a discussion of
lifestyle, proceeding from there to the ideas of optimal leisure lifestyle
and the discretionary time commitment. The basic concepts having thus
been set out, I discuss the lack of appeal of much work (even though it
must be done for society, and most people need the money it brings), while
contrasting it with the intense appeal of the devotee occupations. The
leisure side of this equation is balanced according to the serious leisure
perspective. Next we take up non-work obligation, which may seriously
upset an appealing balance achieved in work or leisure or the two woven
together. In the final section I set out several personal strategies for achieving balance across the domains of work, leisure, and obligation.

Lifestyle

The following definition of *lifestyle* fits well the aims of this book: a
distinctive set of shared patterns of tangible behavior that is organized
around a set of coherent interests or social conditions or both, that is
explained and justified by a set of related values, attitudes, and orienta-

tions and that, under certain conditions, becomes the basis for a separate, common social identity for its participants (Stebbins, 1997b; see also Veal, 1993). At bottom, a lifestyle formed around work, leisure, and obligation rests fundamentally on the ways people allocate their minutes, hours, days, weeks, and so on to activities in the three domains. Generally speaking, in leisure, compared with the other two domains, free time has long been considered a key resource for the individual to manipulate for his or her personal ends. This contrasts with work and non-work obligation, which offer comparatively little temporal flexibility.

More precisely people taking their leisure make *discretionary time commitments*, which are essentially, non-coerced allocations of a certain number of minutes, hours, days, or other measure of time that a person devotes, or would like to devote, to carrying out an activity (Stebbins, 2006b). Such commitments are both process and product. That is people either set (process) their own time commitments (products) or willingly accept such commitments (i.e., agreeable obligations) set for them by others. It follows that disagreeable obligations, which are invariably forced on people by others or by circumstances, fail to constitute discretionary time commitments, since the latter, as process, issue from human agency. In short, this conception of time commitment finds expression in leisure and the agreeable sides of work (which, in effect, are experienced as leisure, see Stebbins 2004a).

Note, however, that we can, and sometimes do, make time commitments to carry out disagreeable activities, whether at work or outside it. Such commitments – call them *coerced time commitments*—are, obviously, not discretionary. Although they are marginal to this book, in the sense that they are negative, they do figure centrally in the present discussion about balancing work, leisure, and obligation. Furthermore, coerced time commitments sometimes turn up in serious leisure, where they may be classified as a kind of "cost" (see chap. 1).

Chronologically speaking, it is common to think in terms of past, present, and future time commitments (discretionary and coerced) at work, leisure, and in the area of non-work obligations. The kinds of time commitments people make help shape their work and leisure lifestyles, and constitute part of the patterning of those lifestyles. In the realm of leisure, the nature of such commitments varies substantially across its three forms. Serious leisure requires its participants to allocate more time than participants in the other two forms, if for no other reason, than that, of the three, it is pursued over the longest span of time. Additionally, certain qualities of serious leisure, including especially perseverance, commitment, effort, and career, tend to make amateurs, hobbyists, and volunteers especially cognizant of how they allocate their free time, the amount of that time they use for their serious leisure, and the ways they accomplish this.

There are many examples. Amateur and hobbyist activities based on the development and polishing of physical skills (e.g., learning how to juggle, figure skate, make quilts, play the piano) require the aspiring entertainer, skater, quilter, and so on to commit a fair amount of time on a regular basis, sometimes over several years, to acquiring and polishing necessary skills. And once acquired, the skills and related physical conditioning must be maintained through use. Additionally some serious leisure enthusiasts take on (agreeable) obligations (Stebbins, 2000a) that demand their presence at certain places at certain times (e.g., rehearsals, matches, meetings, events). But most important, the core activity, which is the essence of a person's serious leisure, is so attractive that this individual very much wants to set aside sufficient time for finding fulfillment in it.

In other words, serious leisure, as mentioned earlier, often borders on being *uncontrollable*; it engenders in its practitioners a desire to pursue the activity beyond the time or the money (if not both) available for it. So, even though hobbies such as collecting stamps or making furniture usually have few schedules or appointments to meet, they are nonetheless enormously appealing, and as such encourage these collectors and makers to allocate, whenever possible, time for this leisure. Moreover, as Stalp (2006) has shown for quilting, the amount of time allocated and when this is done are often negotiated with important others who also have a claim on the participant's hours after work and non-work obligations.

Project-based leisure may be accompanied by similar demands. There are often scheduled meetings or responsibilities, if not both, and though of short range, the condition of uncontrollability may also be a concern. But project-based leisure does not, by definition, involve developing, polishing, and maintaining physical skills, this being one of the key differences in use of discretionary time separating it from serious leisure. Furthermore, with project-based leisure comes a unique sense of time allocation: time use is more or less intense, but in many projects, limited to a known and definite period on the calendar (e.g., when the athletic games are over, when the stone wall is built, when the surprise birthday party has taken place). Indeed, one of the attractions of projects for some people is that no long-term commitment of time is foreseen.

Finally, casual leisure may, in its own way, generate time commitments, as in the desire to set aside an hour each week to watch a television program or participate as often as possible in a neighborhood *kaffeeklatsch*. Further, some casual leisure, famously watching television, is attractive, in part, because it is often available on a moment's notice—call it "spontaneous discretionary time commitment"; it can fill in gaps between discretionary and coerced time commitments, and in the process, stave off boredom. Additionally, casual volunteering commonly has temporal requirements, as in joining for the weekend an environmental clean-up crew, serving on Thanksgiving Day free meals to the poor, and collecting money for a charity by going door-to-door or soliciting on a street corner.

In shaping their leisure lifestyles, people blend and coordinate their participation and allocation of free time in one or more of the three forms. In this regard, some people try to organize their free time in such a way that they approach an *optimal leisure lifestyle* (OLL). The term refers to the deeply rewarding and interesting pursuit during free time of one or more substantial, absorbing forms of serious leisure, complemented by judicious amounts of casual leisure or project-based leisure or both. People find optimal leisure lifestyles by partaking of leisure activities that individually and in combination enable them to realize their human potential, leading thereby to self-fulfilment and enhanced well-being and quality of life (Stebbins, 2000b). I will return to OLL in the concluding section of this chapter.

Work: Non-devotee and Devotee

Poor working conditions, whether social or physical, can amount to a cost so poignant that it overrides love for the core activity, thus forcing the worker into another occupation or, if circumstances permit, early retirement. A news release describes just this plight facing teachers in the Mobile, Alabama area (Havner, 2007), who are increasingly fed up with paperwork, student disciplinary problems, and the like. In another example, baby boomer physicians in Canada typically work such long hours that they become prone to mistakes and burnout, with a corresponding loss of devotion for their line of work (Boesveld, 2007, p. A10). But in true occupational devotion the good conditions prevail on a reasonably regular basis; the bad ones, though seen as costs, being nevertheless outweighed by the first. In brief, occupational devotion is only possible when working conditions are defined as, *on balance*, favorable.

Note, however, that some people like their work, primarily because they enjoy the people with whom they work, often talking informally with them as they go about the various tasks that constitute their jobs or socialize with them on official breaks. In addition, or alternatively, they may like the clients or customers they meet. For these workers, who are not occupational devotees, it is not the nature of the work itself that draws them to it (the work is uninteresting), but the social life that goes with it. Yet, at bottom, this social life is not work at all, but leisure seized in the interstices of free time found on the job, even while such leisure helps make palatable the job itself (Stebbins, 2007d). Indeed, these work ties may extend into the zone of free time well beyond the place of work, as when friends there get together during an evening at a restaurant or an afternoon on the golf course.

Still it is questionable how many people who are bored with their work tasks though pleased with the friends or customers they meet on the job would perform the work for no pay, as leisure. Or how many look forward to going to work after the weekend or equivalent period of time off? Or would they recommend their job as a lifelong career for their children? And what about a fourth measure: are the core activities so attractive as to erase the line between work and leisure (devotee work)? It fails, too, because the humdrum, if not downright unpleasantness, of the core job remains, giving it a decidedly obligatory and chore-like character.

Saying that people like their work because they enjoy its social life, is much the same as saying that people like their work because it pays well or provides great fringe benefits. All such rewards of the job are extrinsic, rewards found outside the core tasks themselves. By contrast, occupational devotion roots in intrinsic rewards, in values realized by carrying out the work tasks themselves. There is no doubt that extrinsic rewards of the sort just described get people to accept jobs and come to work to perform them. And we should be thankful that people can be motivated thus, for there is much work to be done, comparatively little of which is capable of generating occupational devotion.

And this is not to say that occupational devotees gain no extrinsic rewards, only intrinsic ones. Although intrinsic rewards are key devotees, too, may enjoy their work colleagues and, relatively rarely it appears, even reap a high rate of pay and benefits. This is the best of all worlds, to be sure, but we shall see later that, as far as work is concerned, this Leibnizian state is all too infrequent. In other words, occupational devotion, as a concept, directs attention to the core activities making up a work role, by proceeding from the assumption that, more than anything else, it is those activities that attract people to and hold them in that role. In short the four criteria just mentioned – erasing the line between work and leisure, yearning to go to work after the weekend, recommending the work to one's children, and being willing to do the work without pay (as leisure)—serve as reasonably accurate and valid measures of occupational devotion.

Are they paid so they may work? No. Most people, following the obverse thrust of this question, work so they may be paid. And they have to make money or otherwise gain their means of subsistence. In the main, only the independently wealthy, as generated by investments or inheritance, and the institutionalized escape this basic requirement of life. For the rest, when work is uninteresting, but still decently remunerative, workers can at least sustain life and, with whatever money that is leftover, enjoy a bit the smorgasbord of consumerist opportunities that the commercial world lays out before them. A lifetime of uninteresting work is a high price to pay for economic survival and some spending cash, but many a modern worker enters into just this bargain with his educational qualifications and personal standards for occupational success.

When work is highly attractive, however, this conventional orientation toward it and its remuneration often gets stood on its head. Still, the relationship of remuneration to devotee work is complicated, as is evident in the different economic situations that devotees live in or strive to live in. This issue will be taken up in chapter 7. In the meantime we turn to leisure.

Leisure

In conceptualizing quality of life, I use the subjective "want-based" approach (as opposed to the objective "social indicators" approach). The want-based approach consists of four components: "a sense of achievement in one's work, an appreciation of beauty in nature and the arts, a feeling of identification with one's community, a sense of fulfillment of one's potential" (Campbell, Converse & Rogers, 1976, p. 1).

Where does the serious leisure perspective fit in this scheme? Of the three forms, serious leisure, itself, meets best the four components. The first—sense of achievement—is evident in serious leisure from what was said earlier about its rewards of personal enrichment, self-expression, group accomplishment and contribution to the maintenance and development of the group as well as its qualities of career, effort, benefits, and perseverance that people can routinely find here. The second component, which refers to appreciation of beauty in nature and the arts, is found in such serious leisure forms as the outdoor activities and artistic pursuits, including backpacking, cross-country skiing, sculpting, and playing string quartets. Third, all serious leisure has links with the wider community, if in no other way, than through the social worlds of its participants. Additionally however, many serious leisure activities relate directly to the larger community, as through artistic performances by amateurs, interesting displays by hobbyists (of, for example, stamps, model trains, show dogs), and needed services by volunteers. Sense of fulfilment of potential—the fourth component—comes primarily from experiencing the reward of self-actualization, but also, to a certain extent, from two qualities of serious leisure, namely, finding a career in the activity and having occasionally to persevere at following it.

These four components can also be realized in many leisure projects, but the good quality of life found there will be more evanescent, and possibly not even as sharply felt, as in the far more enduring pursuit of a serious leisure activity. Casual leisure, too, can help generate a decent quality of life, although primarily through appreciating beauty in nature and the arts (e.g., subtype of sensory stimulation) and identifying with one's community (e.g., subtype of casual volunteering). Finally, to arrive at an equally valid want-based conceptualization of quality of life in devotee work, we need, in this statement, only to replace serious leisure with devotee work.

High quality of life, however generated, is a state of mind, which to the extent people are concerned with their own well-being, must be pursued with notable diligence. (Did we not speak earlier of career, agency, and perseverance?) Moreover, high quality of life does not commonly "fall into one's lap," as it were, but is rooted in desire, planning, and patience, as well as a capacity to seek deep satisfaction through experimentation with all three forms of leisure to eventually carve out an optimal leisure lifestyle. Human agency is the watchword here (discussed further in chap. 4). And we will see shortly that leisure educators, leisure/lifestyle counsellors among them, can advise and inform about a multitude of leisure activities that hold strong potential for elevating quality of life, but, in the end, it is the individual who must be motivated to pursue them and develop and stick to a plan for doing this.

What then of well-being? In a positive sociology we privilege the social variety as opposed to its subjective counterpart. Keyes (1998, p. 121) defines *social well-being* as the "absence of negative conditions and feelings, the result of adjustment and adaptation to a hazardous world." For him well-being, though a personal state, is influenced by many of the social conditions considered earlier and incorporated in the serious leisure perspective. Though the relationship is probably more complex than this, for purposes of the present discussion, let us incorporate in the following proposition what has been said in this section to this point: social well-being emanates from a high quality of life, as generated by some combination of serious leisure balanced with one or both of the other two forms.

Still, at least one major question remains: can even a serious leisure activity, though not coerced, engender well-being when it is also engenders certain costs and occupies a marginal status with reference to the three social institutions of work, leisure, and family?[1] The answer is, tentatively, yes it can. For, to the extent that well-being is fostered by fulfillment through life's ordinary activities, research evidence suggests that it is an important by-product of serious leisure (Haworth, 1986; Haworth & Hill, 1992; Mannell, 1993). As additional evidence the respondents in my several studies of serious leisure, when interviewed, invariably described in detail and with great enthusiasm the profound fulfillment they derived from their amateur, hobbyist, and volunteer activities.

All this evidence, however, is at bottom only correlational. No one has yet carried out a properly controlled study expressly designed to ascertain whether long-term involvement in a form of serious leisure actually leads to significant and enduring increases in feelings of well-being. The extent to which serious leisure can generate major interpersonal role conflict for some practitioners—it led to two divorces among the twenty-five respondents in a study of amateur theater (Stebbins, 1979, pp. 81-83; on family conflict in running, see Goff, Flick & Oppliger, 1997)—should be warning enough to avoid postulating an automatic link between serious leisure, on the one hand, and well-being, on the other. And, in final two chapters, I treat of the effects of selfishness in serious and casual leisure. I also have anecdotal evidence that serious leisure activities can generate intrapersonal conflict, such as when people fail to establish priorities among their many and varied leisure interests or among those interests and their devotee work. This implies that even an approach-approach conflict between cherished leisure/work activities may possibly affect unfavorably well-being. Hamilton-Smith (1995, pp. 6-7) says our lack of knowledge about the link between serious leisure and well-being is a major lacuna in contemporary leisure research.

Non-Work Obligation

It was stated in chapter 1 that, whereas obligation is substantially mental and behavioral, it roots, too, in the social and cultural world of the obligated actor. Consequently, we may also speak of a culture of obligation that takes shape around many work, leisure, and non-work activities. What does this culture look like?

The essence of the culture of obligation is the shared sentiment of feeling obliged to engage in a particular activity. Let us look, first, at the disagreeable face of obligation. For example, the mother who laments to a friend that she is getting tired of taking her young son to hockey practice at 6:00 AM three times a week is highly is likely to find a sympathetic ear among other parents saddled with the same responsibility. Or the man who complains to his neighbor about having, once again, to mow the lawn voices his lament anticipating shared sentiment with the listener. Since we all have to carry out at various points in life some disagreeable obligations, we can often empathize with others forced to do the same.

The areas of life in which disagreeable obligation tends to concentrate constitute another facet of this culture. The three types set out in chapter 1 also serve as labels for these areas: unpaid labor, unpleasant tasks, and self-care. Additionally, taking now an institutional approach, much of this obligation falls under the heading of family or domestic life, sometimes both, but with disagreeable communal involvements also being possible. Illustrative of the latter is the feeling that many householders might well have who, in facing possible decline in property values, know they should attend a public community meeting about say, an expressway or halfway house for ex-offenders proposed for their neighborhood. Note here, as well, the power of certain social conditions to frame such obligations, including vested community interests of the not-in-my-backyard variety and the professional authority of city planners.

And, while on the institutional plane, note that disagreeable obligation may also be experienced at work as well as in some leisure. Among the aspects of work that people dislike are certain activities they are required to engage in while there. Some of these may be fatiguing such as lifting heavy objects and standing for long periods of time. Others, though not fatiguing, may be boring or otherwise unpleasant, including diagnosing and treating the common cold in medicine (boring), grading examinations in teaching (boring), and attending to injured young children in emergency medical service (emotionally upsetting).

As for the agreeable side of the culture of obligation, consider the following examples. In each of them the obligated participants also want very much to engage in the activity. Thus, imagine the amateur poet who has accepted an invitation to present some of her works at a local coffee house. Both the poet and the person who extended the invitation are aware of her obligation to perform, once the invitation is accepted. It is likewise for a member of an amateur basketball team whose teammates depend on him to play the next match. The sense of obligation to do this is shared by all concerned. Finally, many volunteers and those whom they serve know well the obligation of the former to be present at the appointed time and place to volunteer as promised.

Staying on the institutional level, note that the culture of obligation is found throughout leisure, whether serious, casual, or project-based. That is, in all three forms people may feel obliged to do something that they also want to do. Yet the institutional location of agreeable obligation is even more complex than this. People can feel pleasantly obliged to engage in leisure activities within the family (e.g., to have a picnic, play a board game with the children, or go out to eat with one's spouse). But there are also many pleasant obligatory activities to be enacted in devotee work, seen in performing as a guest concert pianist with a renowned symphony orchestra, providing expert advice as a counselor in a challenging marital dispute, and repairing string instruments as a self-employed lutier.

It is evident in what has been said in this section that obligation, agreeable or not, is also relational, or social. We are not only obliged to undertake certain activities we are also obliged to the individuals who have an interest in them. All the foregoing examples, with the possible exception of mowing the lawn, presuppose the presence of one or more other people who depend on the obligated person to honor his commitment. There is thus a personal tie, a relationship of some duration, between what Cuskelly and Harrington (1997) call "obligees" (e.g., feel they must help a friend or a nonprofit group) and "role dependees" (e.g., young members of a family participating in an activity, for which, to ensure its survival, a parent must volunteer). Again, returning to the conditional level of analysis, we must also, for a complete explanation, inquire into the structural and cultural arrangements underlying this obligation for the role dependee. Is it ultimately caused by a failure of municipal support for the activity, a sudden surge in its popularity, a shortage of qualified personnel to provide it, or a combination of these factors and others?

Finding Balance

What does "balance" mean, when applied to everyday living? In the common sense it seems to refer to "spending more time with family" (see epigraph to this chapter), having more leisure time ("getting a life"), gaining some measure of freedom from unpleasant obligations (escaping the "rat race"), and similar adaptive strategies. In positive sociology, the answer to this question is much more subtle: people may find balance in work, leisure, and obligation by crafting a lifestyle that encompasses these three and that is endowed with substantial appeal. Everyone who is working has some kind of lifestyle bridging these domains. But it is also true that many people have lifestyles they would sooner be rid of, which as the epigraph to this chapter indicates, is a goal they (Canadians in this instance) believe is next to impossible to achieve. How, then, to generate an appealing, balanced lifestyle spanning the three domains? This would be Aristotle's good life, often reached when people abandon some major aspects of their present unappealing lifestyle.

In broadest terms finding an appealing lifestyle hinges on discretionary time commitment. More particularly it hinges, in part, on committing more hours to the activities one likes most, while subtracting hours from those one likes less or flatly dislikes. Understandably this kind of balancing is easiest to accomplish in the domain of leisure, where by definition people stay away from unappealing activities. Even here, however, some activities are more difficult than others to abandon on a whim. So the young male can, at the last moment, tell his friends that the weekend "pub crawl" no longer excites him and that, from hereon, they can continue their escapades without him. But the actress, having grown tired of community theater as performed in her city, can only comfortably announce that, next season, she will be unavailable for roles. She cannot, without great social cost, quit midway through preparation for an upcoming play in the present season her role in that play, for to do so would leave many associates in a lurch and spoiling immensely their serious leisure.

So an appealing, balanced lifestyle may be reached, in part, by tinkering with the balance of leisure activities, spending more time in some while cutting back time spent in others. But, if the person suffering from an imbalance in lifestyle has little free time, then a solution to this problem must be found by redeploying commitments in the other two domains. In one sense, anyway, decisions about which activities to commit less time to in these areas of life are more subtle and difficult than in the domain of leisure. For, the first two domains are loaded with obligations that may, at least at first glance, appear absolutely fixed.

Let us look first at work. The disagreeable obligatory requirements of the job are probably, in most instances, difficult to change. If you are a taxi driver, server in a restaurant, or packer in a warehouse and you hate driving cars, waiting on diners, or filling and taping boxes, you must face the fact that little hope exists for changing these core activities. These are central and immutable features (social conditions) of the taxi, warehousing, and restaurant industries. Nevertheless there are some options. For instance, driving taxis and serving diners usually need not be done as full-time work. Given this option could the driver's or the server's household get along on a part-time wage? Two, if the answer to this question is no, might the breadwinner find a second part-time job consisting of fewer unpleasant obligations?

This brings up the thorny issue of the amount of money a person needs for an agreeable work-leisure-obligation lifestyle. The strategies presented next presume that people seeking an attractive balance in these three domains do not judge their social value as individuals by "what they are worth," by the amount of wealth they have amassed. With such a goal scaling back on opportunities to make ever more money is out of the question. Yet, for most people, this is not their first option, while for those whose social value is measured exclusively in monetary terms, it is no option at all.

We have no scientific data on how many people in modern society judge their social value primarily in pecuniary terms. Although I suspect that their number is far from negligible, I also suspect that those who estimate their worth in other ways are noticeably more common. When it comes to abandoning activities fraught with disagreeable obligations for activities blessed with agreeable ones or with no obligations whatsoever, this latter group has some choices. Put otherwise they may choose among some viable strategies.

Strategies for Balance

During my immersion over the past forty-five years as theorist and researcher in the domains of work and leisure (I started out studying jazz musicians as workers), I have informally observed or read about a variety of ways by which people search for agreeable balance in life's activities. These ways are treated of here as "strategies." The six discussed below —and I make no claim that this list is exhaustive—are presented in no particular order of importance. They are (1) voluntary simplicity; (2) hiring out/ignoring obligations; (3) work reduction; (4) devotee work; (5) retirement; and (6) leisure. Be aware that people seeking balance across the three domains may well employ more than one strategy.

Voluntary Simplicity

The spirit of voluntary simplicity energizes a growing social movement today which goes by the same name. In a book entitled *Voluntary*

Simplicity Duane Elgin (1981), who was heavily influenced by Gandhi, writes that, among other things, it is

> a way of living that accepts the responsibility for developing our human potentials, as well as for contributing to the well-being of the world of which we are an inseparable part; a paring back of the superficial aspects of our lives so as to allow more time and energy to develop the heartfelt aspects of our lives.

The voluntary simplicity movement, which also goes by the denominations of, among others, "simple living" and "creative simplicity," was launched in the mid-1930s with an article written by Richard Gregg (See Elgin, 1981, pp. 297-298, for bibliographic information on the several reprinted versions of this article). Still, the quotations below suggest that need for the movement is centuries old:

> *Better is an handful with quietness, than both the hands full with travail and vexation of spirit—Ecclesiastes 4:6*

> *Half our life is spent trying to find something to do with the time we have rushed through life trying to save—Will Rogers, Autobiography*

As a practical strategy voluntary simplicity may be seen as cutting back on something held by a person to be unnecessary. True simple livers —people ideologically motivated by the movement to create a lifestyle based as fully as possible on the principles of voluntary simplicity—go much farther than a single practice, exemplified in driving a compact car instead of a sport utility vehicle or growing their own vegetables instead of buying them at the supermarket. Rather voluntary simplicity may be pursued in degrees ranging from downsizing the family automobile or growing vegetables to a more completely self-sufficient existence consisting of, among other things, walking and using public transit, making one's own clothing, living in a home no larger than absolutely necessary, and resorting wherever possible to do-it-yourself to meet all domestic obligations. For the purposes of this book voluntary simplicity refers to this entire range of practices leading to a more or less simpler lifestyle than before.

As a balance strategy finding a measure of simplicity opens up the possibility of lessening dependence on the paying job as a whole or on some of its key obligations. One might ask, "Should I need to earn $100,000 annually, were I to drive a cheap, economical car or reduce the size of my house or apartment?" Or "should I need such a job were I to do my own yard work rather than meet this obligation by hiring a costly commercial service?" Voluntary simplicity enables people to live on a reduced income, commonly achieved by, in some way, decreasing the amount of money they allot to managing their non-work obligations.

Hiring Out/Ignoring Obligations

Still, doing one's own yard work, may also be disagreeable. It is likewise with most of the diverse tasks that come with owning a home and running a household. This way of implementing voluntary simplicity is not everyone's cup of tea. So, then, in the interest of a better work/leisure/obligation balance, why not pay someone to do some of these chores, or given sufficient resources, all of them? Granted, adoption of the next strategy, reducing hours of work, is likely to result in a reduction of income, as can taking a new job that enables a level of occupational devotion missing in the old one.

One partial, though not always, feasible solution to this dilemma is to ignore the obligations. But, on the one hand, what would the neighbors say should the grass grow too high, what of the health implications should household dust accumulate, what about the social consequences should the economizing person wear rumpled, unpressed clothes to work? For personal or cultural reasons or both, some obligations are difficult, if not unwise, to ignore. On the other hand, simple livers might just avoid spending money or time on washing their car, attending important community meetings, writing thank-you letters, sending greeting cards, and the like, with little concern for the social consequences of these. In the end deciding to honor many of our non-work obligations boils down to individual choice and whether we can live with the consequences when the obligations are ignored. In any case either ignoring obligations or hiring someone to fill them constitutes another strategic approach to finding balance.

Work Reduction

Reducing work refers to cutting back on the number of hours of employment, and as such, includes shifting to part-time work. Although voluntary simplicity may include reducing working hours, as was noted in the preceding two sections, work reduction can be a balance strategy of its own. It is not necessarily tied to the ideals of simple living. It also comes in many forms. For example the worker might decide (the boss willing) to work forty hours a week rather than fifty. Or he or she might opt for a longer annual vacation period, assuming in this instance that this person controls to some extent the length of holiday (e.g., as in self-employment, underuse of officially allotted holidays). And some people cut their working hours in half or a third at one job, but then add working hours through another part-time job they like better.

The work being considered here is non-devotee work, work that people are happy enough to abandon, in whole or in part, as long as without it, they can maintain a personally acceptable standard of living. When infused with the spirit of voluntary simplicity, the monetary cost of that standard of living is now significantly reduced. But, with or without simplistic goals, why stay employed more than is necessary in a job that lacks appeal, if it is not downright odious? In other words, why not balance life by freeing oneself as much as possible from the gloomy grip of work. Of course, this strategy cuts back on the need to earn money under duress and, as a consequence, frees up some of the time spent making this money. Still, it also raises the question of what to do with that new found time. We examined this question in our discussion of the strategy of obligation, and will consider it again in the section on leisure.

Devotee Work

This strategy centers on finding devotee work, on achieving balance in a lifestyle in which the individual already has a job, albeit of the non-devotee variety. At least two sub-strategies are possible. One is to quit the present non-devotee position to take up employment that inspires occupational devotion. In a rare study of this personal transition, Mellor (2006), using a small sample of Canadian teachers and lawyers who had grown disenchanted with their professional posts, explored how they found devotee work, often work vastly from their former jobs. Thus one former high school teacher joined his wife in the occupation of hog farming. A lawyer in Mellor's sample left her law practice to become a wealth management consultant.

I know of no data on the frequency of such occupational change, and it is probably true that more people would like make such change than have the courage, opportunities, or resources—the facilitating personal and social conditions—to do it. People in the fine and entertainment arts who "quit their day job" to take up full-time work in their art exemplify this strategy. Furthermore leaving a job that lacks the six criteria of occupational devotion for one that meets them often entails a significant reduction in salary, Mellor found. Nazareth (2007, pp. 92-99) refers to this sort of job shifting as "opting out," and she provides numerous Canadian and American examples of her own, many of them women with families.

The second sub-strategy for people seeking balance through the domain of work is to try to transform their present non-devotee jobs into ones leading to occupational devotion. This, however, is often easier said than done. For one, in looking at the six criteria, the core occupational activity must be profound enough to meet them. Thus, the core activities of unskilled and semiskilled work, by definition, fail on most, if not all, of these six, thereby rendering impossible such transformation. In contrast a finishing carpenter (skilled worker) might, for example, abandon his job in tract housing or standardized apartment construction to take up one in custom building. Here there is comparatively more variety and opportunity for innovation and independent judgment. Rosenberg and Fliegel (1965, pp. 156-157) report from their interviews with painters that these artists lamented that attempting to make a living in commercial art was stultifying, among other problems, which drove them to renounce its financial security in favor of the artistic freedom of self-fulfilling "pure" art.

Turning to a different scenario, people already working in a position that has the potential to generate occupational devotion might try to bring it more into line with the six criteria than it presently is. Perhaps the worker can gain greater personal control over execution of its core activities, acquire more scope for her own creativity, increase variety, obtain better environmental conditions for the work, or a combination of these. As I have already observed, bureaucratic structure, when elaborated beyond a minimal level, undermines occupational devotion. Therefore reducing paperwork and organizational complexity can also help develop (or restore) a devotee position, which may, however, be asking the impossible in an expanding organization.

Retirement

Retirement, in positive sociology, refers to people intentionally leaving work as their means of livelihood. These days, in this sense of the word, many people retire between ages 55 and 65, even while some retire earlier and others later. In all instances, because we are discussing the search for balance, retirement is here intentional; it is for them a strategy for finding that balance. People forced to retire by statute, mental or physical disability, lay-off policies, and the like are not leaving their employment with the hope that doing so will improve their lifestyle. Granted some of this latter group may, for instance, be able to exploit the structural arrangement of statutory retirement, waiting to this point to leave with enhanced pension or savings and a broader set of opportunities for putting some needed balance into their lives.

Some intentional retirees plan, albeit at times unrealistically, for their lifestyle after work. Leisure is commonly at the center of such planning, though a proportion of this group will also have to confront at this time various non-work obligations (actual and anticipated). How often have we heard near-retirees proclaim that, in retirement, they will golf, travel, volunteer, or putter happily around the house? Less elated about retiring, however, are those who know little about what they will do with their new freedom, saying only that not having to work is going to be a tremendous relief. Retirement also offers them a chance to find balance, but they cannot say, or say yet, how that balance will be reached.

In short, intentional retirement, as a balance strategy, appears for the typical worker without realistic plans for leisure and obligation to be a kind of lifestyle half-way house. This person must still find an appealing leisure lifestyle, even if it turns out to be less than optimal. But, for retirees in their sixties, time, energy, and sometimes money may start to run out. In other words people who have failed to develop some sort of substantial leisure interest during their working years, may well find themselves at their wits end in retirement, as they try to identify something interesting to do. In particular, learning most serious leisure activities takes a minimum of several months before reaching the point where they are experienced as rewarding. Learning to a satisfying level how to paint, play golf, or play a musical instrument or developing the necessary skills for a craft normally require at least a couple of years of steady application. This is why some pre-retirement counseling includes the recommendation that workers develop a few serious leisure interests well before the day they punch out for the last time.

The nature of retirement also depends on the personal condition of health and the social condition of financial resources. Some people, in part because they can work, avoid retirement because they also have no significant savings or pension. Others retire, though they do this with so little money to live on that their leisure opportunities are severely limited. And even if money is no problem health may be. A retired man who has the money and a passion for golf, but who also has debilitating arthritis is now barred from this leisure activity. Old age is commonly filled with all sorts of maladies that force many in this category out of their favorite leisure interests and consequently into others they may (at least at first) prefer less. In the next chapter we return to retirement as a phase of the life course.

The Centrality of Leisure

These five strategies for finding balance across the three domains all relate in one way or another to leisure. Voluntary simplicity frees time for leisure, as does hiring the enactment of obligations, reducing the number of hours worked, and going into retirement. Devotee work, it is true, focuses the worker's attention on the paying job, often cutting into a portion, for some devotees, even all, of the time that might be otherwise used for leisure. But, then, devotee work *is* essentially serious leisure, with the added advantage that the worker gets remunerated for it.

Given that, in pursuing either serious leisure or project-based leisure, participants make many contributions to the community (the "world" in the earlier quotation by Elgin) and that these two forms offer two avenues for realizing human potential, it is reasonable to interpret participation in such leisure as consistent with the principles of voluntary simplicity. Note, however, that since its adherents also espouse many other principles, this way of living is by no means identical to a life dominated by serious leisure. Nevertheless, the two do share the common ground of encouraging and fostering self-fulfillment through realizing individual human potential and contributing to the well-being of the wider community. For the typical, true devotee of voluntary simplicity, this also often requires paring down work activity, where such activity generates more money than needed for a simple lifestyle while using time that could be spent in self-fulfilling leisure.

In setting out the essence of a proper simplistic lifestyle, Elgin's definition marginalizes, if not depreciates, casual leisure ("paring back of the superficial aspects of our lives"), while championing, in effect, serious and project-based leisure. This conception squares, in part, with the serious leisure perspective (Stebbins, 2006a), since it portrays both the serious and the project-based forms as offering their participants the highly valued possibility of self-fulfillment. But, as set out in chapter 1, the serious leisure perspective also paints casual leisure in attractive colors. For, in contradistinction to the evanescent, hedonic character of casual leisure, it also generates several enduring benefits. They include serendipitous creativity and discovery in play, regeneration from prior intense activity, and development and maintenance of interpersonal relationships.

Paring down the superficial aspects of life is different, then, from eliminating them. In fact, as casual leisure, these aspects are possibly less superficial than Elgin claims. The preceding discussion of the benefits from such leisure supports this point.

Let us turn next to another implication of Elgin's conception of voluntary simplicity. It is that, in effecting a lifestyle truly consistent with the tenets of voluntary simplicity, enthusiasts for this lifestyle also appear destined both to increase their list of non-work obligations and to reduce the amount of free time in which "heartfelt" leisure may be pursued. Consider that living simply might require a person to, for instance, walk and use public transit (in lieu of driving a car), take recyclable trash to a recycling depot (in lieu of sending it to the municipal landfill), grow vegetables or bake bread (in lieu of buying these items at a supermarket), and acquire and use wood for home heating (in lieu of purchasing gas or oil for this purpose). Some of these simple living obligations might well be seen by some folks as pleasant, as essentially leisure, including tending a garden, baking bread, and even chopping wood for home heating. But all such activities take time, which is to be found in a person's weekly hours of free time. But when the activity is disagreeable, this robbing of Peter to pay Paul cuts into the hours that could be used for self-fulfilling free-time activities. It also cuts into time for casual leisure, consequently weakening access to, or the experience of, the previously mentioned benefits it can offer, besides leaving fewer of these activities for rounding out an optimal leisure lifestyle. What is more, people, to the extent they are absorbed with both work and non-work obligations, now have, when it comes to organizing their daily lives, significantly less room for maneuver.

Conclusion: Finding an Optimal Leisure Lifestyle

The preceding pages in this chapter channel the issue of balance toward the leisure domain. With the exception of devotee work (considered separately below), the strategies just examined have the effect of cutting back on disagreeable work and non-work obligations, such that greater scope remains in a person's life for leisure, for additional positive activities. Given the effects of the Information Age, one consequence of which is to reduce the significance of work for many people (c.f., Rifkin, 1995; Aronowitz & DiFazio, 1994), they will have to confront, often for the first time, what they really want to do in their free time. Casual leisure, as respite, was the most common trade-off when work ruled their lives. But, now, with fewer hours on the job and less interesting and more stressful work to do while there, these people could well become interested in searching for more substantial leisure than they had heretofore. Certainly they have reached a point in life where pursuing an optimal leisure lifestyle is a realistic option, where they may become their own agents in enhancing their own personal well-being.

People searching for an OLL strive to get the best return they can from use of their free time. What is considered "best" is, of course, a matter of personal definition, and quality of OLL is predicated, in part, on a person's awareness of at least some of the great range of potentially available leisure possibilities. Thus people know they have an OLL when, from their own reasonably wide knowledge of feasible serious, casual, and project-based leisure activities and associated costs and rewards, they can say they have enhanced their well-being by finding their best combination in two or three of the forms.

So people enjoying an optimal leisure lifestyle are usually conscious of other appealing casual, serious, and project-based leisure activities, but nonetheless sufficiently satisfied with their present set to resist abandoning them or adopting others. Still, this might well change in the future, as an activity loses its appeal, the person loses his or her ability to do it, or new activities gain attractiveness. From what I have observed in my own research, people with OLLs seem to sense that, at a given point in time, if they try to do too much, they will force a hectic routine on themselves, risk diluting their leisure, and thereby become unable to participate fully in what they are enamored of.

Leisure education plays a prominent role here. Without some kind of instruction or reading on the nature and types of serious, casual, and project-based leisure, most people are unlikely to acquire the information they need to choose the complement of activities that would compose their OLL. Fortunately, such courses are ever more common, many being offered these days as lifestyle courses in continuing education programs or private counselling agencies, while various books (Leitner & Leitner, 1994; Stebbins, 1998a; Olson, 2006) now provide detailed information on this way of taking leisure.

Optimal leisure lifestyle is a new concept in the study of leisure. Its strength is that it examines, not leisure activities—the usual approach in leisure studies—but leisured individuals who pursue serious, casual and project-based leisure activities within one or more social worlds and combine these activities to their advantage and satisfaction over their typical day, week, month, season, year, and stage in the life cycle. Looking at annual combinations, for example, my research shows that many amateurs in Canadian football find that combination, in part, by playing rugby during the off-season and, for some, going in for ice hockey during the winter (Stebbins, 1993). Moreover, the mix of activities changes over a person's life course, varying with such factors as age, sex, and health as well as occupational demand, socioeconomic status, and place of residence. Yet emphasis here is always on the individual and human agency, as he or she shapes and reshapes an OLL; draws on available social, educational, and monetary resources; and in serious leisure, finds careers and participates in social worlds.

The life course offers a particularly fruitful framework for studying OLL. The penchant among youth for physically active casual and serious leisure gradually gives way with advancing age to a preference for more sedentary interests and, for some, leisure projects. It is possible that systematic study of OLL will reveal that, during this transition, the balance among the three forms of leisure changes for many people, with older people spending more time enjoying the casual form vis-à-vis the other two. Activities like watching television, going for a walk, and chatting with friends tend to replace more enervating ones such as cycling, hunting, mountain hiking, and even event volunteering.

The typical week is another important time frame for studying OLL. Consider, for instance, the different leisure patterns available to people who work at night, during the day, or on weekends. Activities like sunbathing and daytime bird watching are largely out of the question for night workers, while day workers, at least those in cities, generally miss out on the after-hours bar and restaurant life that vibrates in the wee hours of the morning. And weekend workers, though unable to participate in many Saturday and Sunday picnics, sports events, continuing education workshops, and the like, compete weekdays with relatively few patrons at the swimming pools, ski hills, library tables, and a variety of other facilities.

It is expected that, in the twenty-first century, OLL will vary across the life course more than ever, primarily because the ebb and flow of occupational and non-work responsibilities (e.g., oscillation between part-time and full-time work, temporary unemployment, early retirement, do-it-yourself obligations) will be more unpredictable. Moreover, for a significant part of the population, a decline in interesting work will occur, paralleled by a rise in job-related stress. For these reasons, too, leisure, compared with work, will assume ever greater importance, an attitude sure to elevate the importance of OLL. Much as when people once tried to maximize the benefits they could derive from work, they will increasingly try to do this with leisure, finding as they succeed certain benefits common to both spheres.

What about casual leisure in this combination? It is important to keep it in proper perspective. In the several studies I have conducted on serious leisure activities, many a respondent mentioned his casual leisure, even though that person was being interviewed about a hobby or an amateur or volunteer pursuit (e.g., Stebbins, 2005b, pp. 120-128). And understandably so. An optimal leisure lifestyle includes an appealing balance of the two forms, a point that is sometimes easy to forget in the zealous promotion of serious and project-based leisure. For instance, one of the favorite casual pastimes of many of the interviewees was engaging in what might be called "leisure shoptalk": spirited sessions of sociable conversation about their pursuit held with likeminded enthusiasts. More generally, serious leisure, for instance, typically demands significant energy and concentration, two patently exhaustible resources. If and when exhaustion sets in and some free time remains, one type or another of casual leisure is sure to be sought as a complement. Chances are good, too, that it will be television.

Where does devotee work fit in the formula of optimal leisure lifestyle? Since the first is still work, despite its serious leisure-like features, it must be considered separately. Occupational devotees may well seek to optimize their leisure, even though there is sure to be less of it compared with many other kinds of workers. After all, as will be explained in chapter 7, there is here a strong desire to go to work and to work at the highly attractive core activities found in it, an orientation that inevitably cuts into leisure time and, likely, even the time given to meeting non-work obligations. Thus, for this comparatively small group of fortunate souls, the possibility exists of having the best of both the world of work and that of leisure in what may be called an *optimal positive lifestyle* (OPL). The best in positiveness – defined as both an upbeat attitude toward life and a rewarding level of participation in leisure and devotee activities—that most people may strive for is an OLL, even while the occupational devotee has the opportunity to reach a broader positive existence though an OPL.

Note

1.   On the marginality of serious leisure, see chapter 7 of this book and Stebbins (1979). The costs of serious leisure were covered in chapter 1 of the present book.

4

Personal Development

"Why should society feel responsible only for the education of children, and not for the education of all adults of every age?"—Erich Fromm

"The object of education is to prepare the young to educate themselves throughout their lives."—Robert M. Hutchins

Personal development is another key concept in positive sociology. In this perspective such development refers to positive growth of the individual as a person and a personality, to the realization of that individual's potential as this process unfolds in the socio-cultural milieu . of the day. From the positive perspective and in relation to these forces and arrangements, this growth is seen as substantially directed by the individual. That is, the individual is a main agent in shaping his or her personal development.

On the sociological plane, one central component of personal development is finding and pursuing a formative career in a work role or a leisure role or both. We find such a career in devotee work, serious leisure, but not in casual or project-based leisure.[1] Accordingly, we start this chapter with a discussion of formative career in devotee work and serious leisure, stressing the rewards and self-fulfillment that spring from it and the person's agency in making his or her career what it is. Next, this idea of career is related to the larger concept of life course, wherein, starting as early as adolescence, personal development may extend well into old age. I discuss both formal and informal education and their relationships to adult education and to lifelong and self-directed learning. I also examine the role of the Internet as well as that of digital technology. Next, we consider a second key component of personal development: achieving it through positive relationships. Finally I look at positive emotion and its role in the developmental process.

Formative Career

A *formative career* is the individual's sense of continuous, positive, personal development as it unfolds over the years. It is a subjective concept (Stebbins, 1970), two major components of which are the leisure career and that of devotee work. Of these two the first is the more foundational, since a large majority of today's devotee occupations actually owe their existence, in one way or another, to one or more serious leisure precursors (Stebbins, 2004a, pp. 73-75).

A *leisure career* is the typical course, or passage, of a type of amateur, hobbyist, or volunteer that carries the person into and through a leisure role and possibly into and through a work role. The effect of human agency in a person's career in serious leisure (and possibly later in occupational devotion) is evident in his or her acquisition and expression of a combination of the special skills, knowledge, and experience associated with the core activities. Furthermore, as mentioned in chapter 1, every serious leisure career both frames and is framed by the continuous search for certain rewards, a search that takes months, and in some fields years, before the participant consistently finds deep fulfilment in the chosen amateur, hobbyist, or volunteer role or sometimes later on, in a variety of devotee work. Leisure career, thus considered, is, it should now be clear, a major source of motivation to continue pursuing the activity.

The essence of any career, whether in work, leisure, or elsewhere, lies in the temporal continuity of the events and activities associated with it. Moreover, we are accustomed to thinking of this continuity as one of accumulating rewards and prestige, as progress along these lines from some starting point, even though continuity may also include career retrogression. In the worlds of sport and entertainment, for instance, athletes and artists may reach performance peaks early on, after which the prestige and rewards diminish as the limelight shifts to younger, sometimes more capable practitioners. Serious leisure careers have been empirically examined in my own research and that of Baldwin and Norris (1999); Hastings, Kurth, and Schloder (1996); Heuser (2005); McQuarrie and Jackson 2002; and Bartram (2001).

Career continuity may occur predominantly within, between, or outside organizations. Careers in organizations such as a community orchestra or hobbyist association only rarely involve the challenge of the "bureaucratic crawl," to use the imagery of C. Wright Mills. In other words, little or no hierarchy exists for them to climb. Nevertheless, the amateur or hobbyist still gains a profound sense of continuity, and hence career, from his or her more or less steady development as a skilled, experienced, and knowledgeable participant in a particular form of serious leisure and from the deepening satisfaction that accompanies this kind of personal growth. Some volunteer careers are intra-organizational as well.

Still, many amateurs and volunteers as well as some hobbyists have careers that bridge two or more organizations. For them, career continuity stems from their growing reputations as skilled, knowledgeable practitioners and, based on this image, from finding increasingly better leisure opportunities available through various outlets (as in different teams, orchestras, organizations, tournaments, exhibitions, journals, conferences, contests, shows, and the like). Meanwhile still other amateurs and hobbyists, who pursue non-collective lines of leisure (e.g., tennis, painting, clowning, golf, entertainment magic), are free from even this marginal affiliation with an organization. The extra-organizational career of the informal volunteer, the forever willing and sometimes highly skilled and knowledgeable helper of friends and neighbors is of this third type.

The serious leisure participants who stick with their activities eventually pass through four, possibly five career stages: beginning, development, establishment, maintenance, and decline. Nevertheless the boundaries separating these stages are imprecise, for as the condition of continuity suggests, the participant passes largely imperceptibly from one to the next. The beginning lasts as long as is necessary for interest in the activity to take root. Development begins once the interest has taken root and its pursuit becomes more or less routine and systematic. Serious leisure participants advance to the establishment stage once they have moved beyond the requirement of having to learn the basics of their activity. During the maintenance stage, the leisure career is in full bloom; here participants are now able to enjoy to the utmost the pursuit of it, the uncertainties of getting established having been put behind them, for the most part. By no means all serious leisure participants face decline, but those who do, experience it because of deteriorating mental or physical skills. A more detailed description of the career framework and its five stages is available elsewhere (Stebbins, 1992, chap. 5; on hobbies see Stebbins, 1996a).

Life Course

Unlike career, linked as it is to particular roles, life course is much broader, covering numerous roles as they evolve, interweave, and are assumed or abandoned across the lifetime of a person (Bush and Simmons, 1981, pp. 155-157). Furthermore, life course, when viewed sociologically, centers on age-graded roles and generational effects. Thus it has a historical dimension as well as links to social structure based on the status associated with each role. For instance, Fisher, Day, and Collier (1998) observe that old age is uniquely characterized by "generativity," which includes taking on the responsibility of caring for others as effected through such roles as parent, spouse, friend, and grandparent. When not perceived as personal obligation such care may lead to fulfilment in a leisure role. Of all the age periods composing the life course, the third age, or that period of life between age fifty and seventy-five (also known as the age of the "young-old" or "active retirement"), offers the richest opportunity for finding fulfilment (Laslett, 1994). Brooks (2007) and Wuthnow (2007), by contrast, discuss the still, little-understood "odyssey years," or that period after adolescence and before adulthood (roughly ages eighteen to thirty-five) during which people in this category commonly exist in a state of uncertainty with respect to marriage, work, education, family, and quite possibly, even leisure.

Life course is also broader than the related idea of family life cycle, in that the latter is limited to family matters. Additionally, family life cycle, although chronological as career and life course are, is not, however, essentially processual. Process is a continuous series of actions, events, and changes, and in the social sciences, includes the assumption that these actions and the like emerge from, or are influenced by, each other in seamless fashion. Moreover, this influence may have has past (retrospective), present (immediate), and future (prospective) components. Life cycle, on the other hand, deals with historically arrayed, discrete slices of time, often called phases, and within each, events and actions are typically treated of as static. The classic study of leisure and family life cycle is that of Rhona and Robert Rapoport (1975). In short, life course offers a special slant on leisure and social process.

Why Process is Important

The most obvious answer to this question is that human social life is, in significant part, processual, and a complete scientific explanation of that life must of necessity include this aspect of it. More subtly, however, is the fact that careers and life course, as processes, are important because they constitute strong motivational forces. Agency is not only a main source of personal action, it is also the process by which the individual carries out that action. For instance, both success and failure in a career often motivate people to try to build on the first to achieve still more success and do what they can to avoid the second. Concerning life course, people often seem to want, for example, to harmonize personal interests and role obligations. Thus Wearing and Fulagar (1996) concluded from their studies of Australian women that, today, some of them are modifying traditional family roles to put themselves in a position to pursue activities not ordinarily open to females.

Moreover, both career and life course, by dint of their emergent qualities, encourage people to take stock of what has happened up to a certain point in time in a particular career or during one's life. The "life review" (Butler, 1963), said to be common among the elderly, exemplifies stock-taking of the life course variety. It involves returning to past experiences and unresolved conflicts to make new interpretations of both, the aim being to reintegrate them into life as it has since unfolded. Successful reintegration can bring new positive significance and meaning to the life course of the subject and prepare this person for death. Likewise, careers in particular roles seem to encourage at numerous junctures both retrospective and prospective reviews of how they have gone and how they will or may go in the future. Strategizing about how to pursue a career in the present or the future is part of this stock-taking, and to the extent that the observations and possibilities are agreeable, this can be a positive process.

This is as true of leisure roles as it is of non-leisure roles. Still, this observation is probably most valid for serious leisure roles, where over the long term, there are skills and knowledge to develop and apply and experience to accumulate and profit from. The life review in old age could certainly include interpretation of the good and the bad experienced in earlier and even ongoing serious leisure roles.

Retirement planning may be similarly viewed. Workers contemplating retirement, to plan effectively, must first examine their present work and non-work lifestyle and then try to forecast reasonably accurately which aspects of it they would like to continue and which they would like to abandon or change once they are no longer working full time. This includes coming to grips with the nature of the new lifestyle of casual and serious leisure (Greenwald, in press), its financial requirements, and the conditions of personal health of self and others on whom the retiree is dependent or who are dependent on the retiree. A detailed sense of one's past, present, and future needs, interests, and resources is key in effective retirement planning. A survey by Principal Financial Services (2004, p. 4) suggests that as many as half of pre-retirees have not yet planned for their savings in retirement and only one-fourth have tried to calculate how much they must save for this phase of life. Greenwald (2008) observes that, during pre-retirement, they are even less inclined to plan for the leisure facet of their future after work.

Third, for leisure studies specialists interested in research questions best approached through narrative research, both career and life course offer useful frameworks for organizing data from interviews that inquire into people's leisure lives. As above, narratives about leisure would seem to be most commonly collected from enthusiasts who have spent years in a serious leisure activity, who would, it is presumed, have much to recount about their career there and about how that leisure role has meshed with other major roles in their lives. Manning's (1999) work on high-risk narratives gathered from hobbyist adventurers in nature (sea, jungles, mountains, etc.), exemplifies this approach. And Fullagar and Owler (1998), in a narrative study of people with a mild intellectual disability, were, in effect, looking at life course considerations stemming from their respondents' pursuit of leisure in group settings, which the latter qualified as more substantial than the "boring" leisure of entertainment television.

The Role of Contemplation

For purposes of this book, contemplation and reflection are treated as synonyms, both terms referring to the act of intensely thinking about something. When contemplating (reflecting) we place thought on a particular subject at the center of our attention; it is the dominant activity of the moment. As an activity that endures over time, running in length from a few seconds to possibly an hour or more, it is nonetheless largely mental, even though the contemplator may manipulate related objects during this period. Contemplation may be intense and more or less impermeable, as expressed in the phrase "lost in thought," or it may be comparatively permeable, where a person's thoughts are easily interrupted by environmental stimuli.

One type of reflection—*serious leisure as contemplation*—is devoted to solving a problem arising with regard to a serious leisure activity (Stebbins, 2006d). Though this is not play, it is nevertheless uncoerced, in that the activity itself is uncoerced. This kind of reflection occurs when, for example, a participant considers the best training approach for an upcoming marathon, ponders which of two musical instruments to buy or reflects on the pros and cons of a prospective volunteer role. *Contemplation as serious leisure*—a second type—is the classificatory home of reflective activity engaged in for its own sake. This activity is complex, since participants striving to learn how to execute it must acquire special skills and a body of knowledge to go with them. This type, which is sometimes called "meditation," is exemplified by such systems as Yoga, Tai Chi, and Transcendental Meditation. Meditation, or contemplation, in search of spirituality as guided by the Christian religion is a further example. (Doohan, 1990, examines the link between leisure and spirituality, cited in Ouelette, 2003). Some forms of specifically religious meditation, to be effective, require, in addition to knowledge of technique, knowledge of the religious system from which the first receives its inspiration.

Contemplation as serious leisure would seem to be most accurately classified as a hobby of the activity participant variety. Activity participation was described earlier as the classificatory home of noncompetitive, rule-based, pursuits. And there are obviously many rules and procedures comprising the meditative systems mentioned in the preceding paragraph. Further, in every such system, rules abound on how to behave with reference to other people and objects in the settings in which meditation occurs. Contemplation as serious leisure is similar to what Tanquerey (1924) called "acquired contemplation," in contradistinction to "infused contemplation," or that instilled in a person by God.

How does contemplation relate to spirituality? Whatever else it may be, spirituality is, evidently, a mental state, specifically one of profound regard for the spiritual, for the nonmaterial. This is one sense of the concept. For spirituality is also an important product, or outcome, of some, though not all, contemplation. It appears to be, most clearly, a product of certain sessions of casual leisure contemplation as well as all sessions of serious leisure as contemplation. Thus, we might casually think about the vastness, beauty, or purpose of breathtaking scenery, finding in the process, almost accidentally, a kind of spirituality. Whereas the spirituality reached though serious leisure meditation, for example, is part of the intended result of such activity.

In this respect Ouellette and Carette (2004) make a crucial point, namely, that it is important to find time for reflection that fosters personal revitalization achieved by getting to know oneself better. For them the monastery offers an ideal environment for pursuing this goal. By the same token, however practical this quest may sometimes be, it is also likely to be experienced as leisure. For personal revitalization is very much akin to what is referred to in leisure studies as "recreation." Through either process we get recharged to carry on with life's obligatory activities. Meanwhile "getting to know oneself" relates closely to self-fulfillment (discussed in chapters 1 and 5) and personal development, to learning what, as individuals, we are capable of, have an aptitude for and possess the background preparation to do. To be sure such learning is practical, but more importantly, it is also, in the end, the ultimate payoff of the various serious leisure pursuits, in general, and the contemplation of these two types, in particular.

Education

Formative careers rest on education, defined broadly for our purposes as developing mental or physical powers, if not both, as this process leads to formation of character or an aspect of it. Education of this sort may be formal; it is given and received in specially designed instructional programs ranging in length from a few hours (e.g., an adult education course on fly tying) to many years (e.g., a doctoral program in sociology). Or the education may be informal; it is given and received outside such programs by way of advice, mentoring, posing questions, on-the-job training, coaching (when not formalized as an organizational program), and self-directed educational activities (e.g., reading, listening, watching), and the like. Nowadays many people use the Internet as a source of informal education, even while formal courses are also available here.[2]

As near as I can tell, for the majority of formative careers, whether based in work, leisure, or both, people in them develop themselves through formal *and* informal education. Indeed it is difficult to imagine a kind of devotee work or serious leisure the preparation for which could only be formal. Yet there are kinds of work and leisure that some enthusiasts pursue with only informal education, among them, collecting, amateur sport, amateur entertainment, do-it-yourself, and certain small businesses of the devotee variety.[3]

Leisure Education

The ideas presented above are consistent with Brightbill's definition of leisure education: "the process of helping *all* persons develop appreciations, interests, skills, and *opportunities* that will enable them to use their leisure in personally rewarding ways" (italics in original, Brightbill, 1961, p. 188). Brightbill wrote about "education for leisure," when leisure was a growing but still only a small part of life. Our interest—and his definition harmonizes well with it–is broader, however; leisure education is an effective adaptation to the modern era, part of education for personal development in which leisure plays a central role. The foregoing statement on career and life course attests this.

Given the passage just quoted, I think it safe to say that, were Brightbill writing today, he would argue that leisure education should be centered, for the most part, on either serious or project-based leisure, if not both. In particular, such education should consist mainly of imparting knowledge about the nature of these two forms, about their costs and rewards, and about how to find and participate in particular leisure activities of this sort. This conception of leisure education intentionally excludes much of casual leisure, on grounds that such leisure, hedonic as it is, requires little or no training or encouragement to engage in it and find enjoyment there.

Since the general public is largely unaware of the concepts of serious and project-based leisure, the first goal of educators for leisure, who when conceived of broadly include counselors, volunteers, and classroom instructors as well as people giving informal advice is to inform their clients or students about the nature and value of these two. Such information is important for anyone searching for an optimal leisure lifestyle. More particularly, such education should be composed of instruction on the nature of serious and project-based leisure, the general rewards (and costs) of such activity, the possibility of finding a leisure career in the first, and the variety of social and psychological advantages that can accrue to the person who pursues either of them (e.g., special identity, attractive routine and lifestyle, organizational belonging, central life interest, membership in a social world). Furthermore some people will need advice on how to get started in the pursuits of interest to them.

Elsewhere, I and others provide information on how to do this in North America (Stebbins, 1998a, chap. 6; Olson, 2006; Leitner & Leitner, 1994), which however, may sometimes be inappropriate for other parts of the world. Thus, to more effectively guide the people they are working with, leisure educators outside North America may have to gather information on how to get started that is specific to their country and local community. Everywhere culturally sensitive leisure education can help ensure smooth passage into, what for most people, is uncharted territory: the world of fulfilling free time (see Cohen-Gewerc & Stebbins, 2007).

Adult Education

Since I have examined elsewhere in detail the link between adult education and leisure (Stebbins, 2001a, pp. 94-102), we need here only consider, in broad terms, this link. This will set the stage for a longer discussion on lifelong learning and the serious leisure perspective. As a guide we will use the definition of adult education prepared by UNESCO:

> Adult education is the entire body of organized educational processes, whatever the content, level and method, whether formal or otherwise, whether they prolong or re-

place initial education in schools, colleges and universities as well as apprenticeship, whereby persons regarded as adult by the society to which they belong develop their abilities, enrich their knowledge, improve their technical or professional qualifications or turn them in a new direction and bring about changes in their attitudes or behavior in the twofold perspective of full personal development and participation in balanced and independent social, economic and cultural development. (UNESCO, 1976, p. 2)

Learning—adult learning in particular—is the object of these educational processes. "Continuing education" often refers to the same processes, although the idea usually connotes furthering a person's education beyond initial education undertaken as preparation for a work role (Jarvis, 1995, p. 29).

In general, and in harmony with the emphasis in leisure education, adult education centers, for the most part, on serious rather than casual leisure. Such education can also be pursued, however, as a leisure project. For instance, amateurs in many arts and scientific fields avail themselves of adult education courses, and in the arts, even whole programs, that further their learning of a serious leisure activity. The same may be said for most of the individual amateur sports (e.g., golf, tennis, racquetball). Still, if we examine all the adult educational programs available in the typical North American city, it becomes clear that they ignore some amateur activities (e.g., handball, rodeo, weight lifting, as well as auto and motorcycle racing and virtually all the entertainment arts, Stebbins, 2001a, p. 97).

Adult education is also, with the exception of collecting, a main avenue for learning hobbies. A great range of making and tinkering activities fill the multitude of North American adult education catalogues, including baking, decorating, do-it-yourself, raising and breeding, and various crafts (for a discussion of the many different hobbies, see Stebbins, 1998a, chap. 3). The same is true for activity participation, which includes such diverse enthusiasms as scuba diving, cross-country skiing, mushroom gathering, and ballroom dancing as well as a few of the hobbyist activities and sports and games (e.g., bridge, orienteering, and the martial arts). On the other hand the liberal arts hobbies are most often acquired purely through self-direction, chiefly by reading. But here, too, we find exceptions, as in the general interest courses offered on certain arts, cultures, philosophies, and histories. Indeed, language instruction is one of the pillars of adult education.

Adult education courses related to volunteerism center mostly in such areas as fund raising, accounting and book-keeping, and management and recruitment of volunteers. To the extent that serious leisure volunteers are involved in these areas, they are likely to be interested in courses bearing on them. Still many career volunteers devote themselves to other tasks, which they learn outside the framework of adult education. That is, the group (club, society, association, organization) in which they serve provides the basic instruction they need to learn further while on the job.

Consonant with Houle's (1961) distinction between learning-oriented and goal-oriented motives for pursuing adult education is the fact that the liberal arts hobbies are the only form of serious leisure where learning is an end in itself. By contrast, amateurs, volunteers, and other hobbyists use educational learning as a means to particular leisure ends, such as producing art, playing sport, collecting objects, or helping others. Sometimes both types of participant enrol in the same course, a pattern that may be especially common in science. Thus, some students in an adult education astronomy course may be liberal arts hobbyists, while others are there to learn about the heavens as background for their research.

Jones and Symon (2001) draw a similar distinction in their exploration of the implications of this difference for governmental policy in Britain. They note that adult education and lifelong learning offer resources oriented toward serious learning for six special groups: the unemployed, unwaged (volunteers), elderly, women, "portfolio workers" (holders of many different jobs over a lifetime), and people with disabilities. Serious leisure offers an involving, fulfilling career to these groups that some of their members once had at work and other members never had there. Contemporary governmental policy in Britain (and, I should like to add, quite likely in all other Western countries) tends to overlook the existence of serious leisure and its implications for personal fulfillment, quality of life, and well-being.

Project-based leisure describes what people are doing when they take one or a few courses, with no intention of further involvement in the subject studied. Many a person has sat through an adult educational course on, say, astronomy, music appreciation, or a genre of history simply for the pure satisfaction of learning something interesting in these areas. Having learned what they set out to learn, they see that "project" as completed, perhaps then moving on to another project.

Self-Directed Learning

Roberson (2005, p. 205) notes the crucial differences between adult education and self-directed learning and then links the second to serious leisure. Drawing on an earlier conceptualization by Lambdin (1997), he says that "self-directed learning is intentional and self-planned learning where the individual is clearly in control of this process." Such learning may be formal (here it would be synonymous with adult education), but most often, it is informal. An important condition is agency, that the learner controls the start, direction, and termination of the learning experience. Both adult education and self-directed learning are types of "lifelong learning." The latter is a broader idea than the first two, summarized by Selman and colleagues (1998, p. 21) as learning done throughout a person's lifetime, "from the cradle to the grave."

Roberson (2005) found that his sample of rural, elderly Americans (in the State of Georgia) took their learning seriously, as they pursued amateur, hobbyist, or volunteer roles. At the same time the respondents also said they "enjoyed" or had "fun" in these learning experiences. Roberson said they were "playful" when involved in them. In fact his findings would seem to lend empirical weight to the importance of the reward of self-gratification, where participants find a combination of superficial enjoyment and deep self-fulfilment.

Application

Education, formal or informal, adult or self-directed, gives the background knowledge needed to pursue a formative career. In some careers of this sort, this knowledge is directly applicable. Thus, the engineer who has learned how to design a bridge, when called upon to do so, applies what she has been taught. The physician, having learned in medical school how to diagnose the common cold, uses this knowledge with patients presenting appropriate symptoms. A hobbyist writer, with a course or two on creative writing under his belt, is now ready to apply what he has learned there in writing a poem or a short story.

Still there are occupational devotees and serious leisure participants (amateurs, hobbyists) who must learn further how to use the knowledge they have acquired. For some of these people this entails developing one or more skills. In other words, for them, application includes practicing, for instance, a golf swing, some musical scales, certain strokes with a calligraphy pen, or the sleight of hand needed for a magician's trick. Others need a special preparatory learning, as opposed to the background learning acquired through formal and informal education. Preparatory learning is exemplified in learning the lines of a role in a play, the course to be run in a marathon, the responsibilities of a volunteer position, or the rules of contract bridge. As with the acquisition of skills such preparation is required in certain kinds of devotee work and serious leisure.

Experience

One of the strengths of the concept of formative career is that it accords a place for experience in devotee and serious leisure activities. Gaining experience in such activities takes time; that is it comes through repeated application of skill, education, and preparatory knowledge. My respondents in the several studies of serious leisure and devotee work that I have conducted over the years often talked about the importance of being experienced in what they did. For them greater experience translated into a smoother, less problematic, more efficient pursuit of both the core and the peripheral activities of their work or leisure than was possible with less experience. In other words experience elevated the positiveness of their participation in these two domains.

But what, in detail, does experience consist of? It consists of familiarity with the usual or typical circumstances and situations in which core activities are pursued, leading to an ever more refined judgment of how to pursue those activities. Experience, itself, is a kind of knowledge, gained as it were on the job, and as such differs from the background and preparatory types. Some experience is the result of conscious retrospective observation and reflection (e.g., post-mortem analyses of a concert, game, speech), whereas other experience is gained subconsciously and expressed in the subtle adjustments seasoned participants automatically make to particular environmental cues. As an example of the latter, I, as a jazz bassist, know from experience when the rhythm section (usually some combination of drums, bass, guitar, and piano) is playing together optimally. My past years in this activity, during which the rhythm has sometimes been optimal and sometimes less so, combine today to tell me how well a given musical group is performing rhythmically and where the problem lies when, in this respect, it is performing poorly. Turning to sport the clever "moves" of seasoned athletes may be traced, in substantial part, to the subtle lessons of past experience.

The Internet and Digital Technology

The Internet bears on all we have covered so far in this chapter. For one, it may be a font of formal or informal educational knowledge, as seen in online courses (formal) and online encyclopedias and specialized websites (informal). Indeed, the Internet is a tremendous resource for self-directed learning, though users must figure out how to differentiate authoritative from non-authoritative sources. Two, the Internet is more than a repository of knowledge, since it also enables pursuit of certain serious leisure activities, for example, online scrabble, poker, and a great variety of games known only in cyberspace (Silverman, 2006, studied serious leisure participants in massive multiplayer online games). Some online serious leisure activities are fraught with moral implications, however, as in the online hobbyist clubs devoted to revealing the nature of locks and the skills of picking them (Muñoz, 2006) and those that promote mate swapping. Three, the Internet offers information (as distinct from education) of practical value in pursuing a career in devotee work or serious leisure. For instance, a professional chemist might go to a website to learn more about a conference he wants to attend. A liberal arts hobbyist might seek books in her area of interest by browsing one or more online book stores.

The digital world is also a source of both formal and informal education. For instance, databases containing entire digitized books and issues of periodicals are available to subscribers, whether organizations and their members or non-organized individuals. Some websites have digital libraries composed of material of interest to subscribers or offered free to the interested public. A wide range of material can now be digitized, including written and printed text; drawings, paintings, and photographs; vocal and instrumental music; plans and blueprints, and videos and films. Use of these documents might, for example, be required in completing a formal assignment in a university course or it might be needed in the informal educational pursuit of a worker, hobbyist, or career volunteer.

Personal and Social Identity

The sixth distinguishing quality of serious leisure (see chap. 1) is that its participants tend to identify strongly with their chosen pursuits. No small wonder. With formative careers, as have just been described, it is inevitable they would come to see themselves, usually proudly, as a certain kind of amateur, hobbyist, or career volunteer. True, self-perception as a particular kind of amateur depends on how far into the career the individual has got. Neophytes—serious leisure participants at the beginning their formative career but intending to stay with the activity and develop in it—are unlikely to identify themselves as true amateurs or hobbyists. To do that, they must believe they are good enough at it to stand out from its dabblers, even while they are comparatively weak vis-à-vis more experienced participants, including in the case of amateurs, the professionals in their field.

Identity has both a social and a psychological side. Thus a person's identity is part of his personality, which in one sense, is a psychological matter. The individual enthusiast's view of self as an ongoing participant in complex leisure activity (serious and project-based forms) is a situated expression of this personal identity. It is based on dimensions like level of skill, knowledge, and experience as well as number and quality of physical acquisitions (e.g., good health, collectibles) and lasting physical products (quilts, paintings) stemming from the leisure. So, a young woman might remark to a new acquaintance that she is a skateboarder, but qualify the image she is projecting by noting that she has only been in the hobby two years. She is a skateboarder and proud of it, but do not look to her, at least just yet, for expert demonstrations of its core activities. This presentation of self to the acquaintance is a sociological matter, however, in that the skateboarder not only wants the other to know about her leisure but also for that person to form an accurate impression of her ability to partake in it.

A person's social identity refers to the collective view that the other people in a particular leisure setting hold of these same levels and acquisitions. It is by social identity, among other ways, that the community (including family, neighbors, friends) places people in social space. So, John not only sees and identifies himself as a coin collector, but also various members of the community identify him this way. The fact that complex leisure offers a distinctive personal and social identity is central to personal development. Moreover it is a point that leisure educators should emphasize. For such an identity is unavailable in casual leisure–the leisure most people know–suggesting therefore that the large majority of people receiving leisure education will find the idea a novelty.

Personal and social identity are blended and elaborated in the concept of role identity. A *role-identity* is a person's "imaginative view of himself as he likes to think of himself being and acting as an occupant of a particular social position or status" (McCall & Simmons, 1978, p. 65). True, in many instances, when viewed from the framework of positive sociology, we might more properly speak of an "activity-identity," since there is no role or the concept of role fits less well. But this caveat having been made, I will, in deference to the authors of role-identity, stay with their original nomenclature. The point to remember is that people not only see themselves in the present in their serious leisure activities and the way they carry them out, they also have an image of what they hope to become and do there in the future. Put otherwise a participant's role-identity brings a special analytic angle to the formative career on which this person has embarked. Such people have plans and hopes for the future of their activities, which give distinctive shape to their careers from the present onward. This outlook is illustrated in the orientation of some of the industrial league baseball players

I interviewed (Stebbins, 1979, pp. 206-210). They saw themselves as good enough to be drafted by one of the major league teams, and consequently during games, were always hoping a scout might turn up to observe.

All that has been discussed in this section applies equally well to occupational devotion, which can be broadly described as serious leisure done for a living. Devotees, too, find personal and social identities in their work activities, and they, too, have plans and hopes for the future in those activities. As in serious leisure these matters of identity bestow a positiveness on the job, helping to make life that much more attractive for the worker.

The Commonwealth Secretariat (2007) has issued a report extolling the virtues "cosmopolitan identities" that people of different nationalities and religions share across these two global, rigid, often fractious divisions. Cosmopolitan identities, which tend to be positive anchors in life, include being parents, fans of a particular sport, music buffs, kinds of hobbyists, devotees in given occupations, and so on. Such interests can be powerful, overriding in certain situations many other categorical placements, many of them demographic. Thus, Stebbins (1976) found that classical musicians were typically far less concerned about the sex, race, and social class of their partners in the ensemble than about their ability to play their instruments. Concerted music is no fun to play—leisure is spoiled—when a key player performs it poorly. We return to this idea in chapter 7 when we look at the role of positiveness as a way of ameliorating social problems.

Positive Relationships

In the framework of positive sociology a *positive relationship* is conceived of as a sustained, agreeable orientation by one person toward another, where this orientation is perceived by both as reciprocated. The positive relationship is an elementary form. It may also be embedded in a group having such ties, such as a club, family, or work unit, in this way endowing these collectivities with their own positiveness. The positive qualifier is necessary because interpersonal relationships are not always of this nature; witness the hate and fear relationships that some people must endure (e.g., tense marriage, hatred between two neighbors) or the relationships of disrespect that torment some pairs of individuals (e.g., two scientists espousing opposing theories, who see each other as too dull to grasp the better explanation, namely, that of the colleague). These negative relationships have no place in a positive sociology, however prevalent they are in many people's lives.

But there can be no doubt that the positive relationships characterizing some marriages and some relationships linking relatives, friends, acquaintances, employers and employees, professionals and clients as well as all mentors and their protégés, to mention a few, are a significant force in both generating personal well-being and contributing to personal development. Although well-being is taken up in detail in chapter 7, let us briefly note here that it is enhanced by positive relationships and by a diversity of interactive processes such as sharing humor, anecdotes, and memories; participating in mutual experiences; pulling through together in difficult times; caring for one another; and sharing useful or interesting information. A main part of the positive side of life is being involved from time to time through processes like these with loved, enjoyable, respected, or in other ways attractive human beings.

How do positive relationships contribute to personal development? They do this in at least four ways. One, people in positive relationships often serve as respected others for one another (Mead, 1934) whose favorable responses to and views of alter help shape the senses of identity and self-worth of both. Two, people in some positive relationships are facilitative agents in the other's leisure activities or devotee work, and in this manner, help make possible for that person positive career development in those spheres of life. Examples include tennis or bridge partners, collaborators in a small business, husband and wife who routinely fish together, and two friends who dine out fortnightly. Three, people in positive relationships may receive psychological support from one another, including encouragement, compliments, admiration, useful advice, willingness to serve as a sounding board, and so on. Four, speaking of support, consider the effect of economic sustenance where, when received in a positive relationship, it may aid personal development. This is illustrated in the classic cases of the working wife whose job sustains both herself and her husband who is a graduate student and the working husband whose income enables his wife to pursue a career as an aspiring painter while avoiding the financial plight of the starving artist.

Still it should be clear that no so-called positive relationship is purely positive. Rather it is only so on balance. For there are, for instance, occasional unpleasant disagreements, health problems, financial setbacks, and external strains (e.g., a sick child for two parents, heavy pressure at the office for the husband, excessive demands by the wife's aging father). Sometimes the negative side of life even forces an end to a positive relationship, as in a divorce, resignation (can no longer tolerate the boss), or falling out (between, say, two friends). It is not my intention in this section to try to provide a complete sociological picture of relationships, but rather, much more particularly, to note that, when positive, they contribute mightily to well-being and personal development. They should, in this state, be seen as a central part of a positive sociology.

I opened this section with the observation that positive relationships are an elementary form, since they may also be interlinked such that they help constitute a primary group, for instance a club, family, or work unit. When this happens these kinds collectivities acquire their own measure of positiveness; they, too, offer positive experiences for their members, which may contribute to the personal development of each. As an example, a soccer player is likely to come away from a game with a sense of being good at the sport, after having received a round of enthusiastic compliments from teammates about that person's commendable scoring prowess during the contest. Moreover, positive recognition contributing to personal development may grace an outstanding member of a large-scale organization. This is illustrated in being voted the season's Most Valuable Player in the league or being honored with the award of Volunteer of the Year, given by the municipal council. The study of these entities with a view to what makes life worth living is still another facet of positive sociology.

Positive Emotion

The sociology of emotion, which sometimes centers on negative expressions, sometimes on positive ones, some times on emotion in general, offers, through its positive focus, another main conceptual basis for a positive sociology. Certainly life is experienced as noticeably agreeable when people feel joy, pride, love, happiness, satisfaction, and other such states. Moreover these states are often part of the experience gained in a positive career, identity, or relationship; the states add significantly to the sense of positiveness felt in these three.

Turner and Stets (2006), in a review of the field of the sociology of emotion, extracted sets of generalizations from the diverse theoretic perspectives that have occasionally concentrated sociological attention on this phenomenon. One of their generalizations bears on identity. It flows from research guided by the symbolic interactionist perspective: "the more an identity is verified by the responses of others, the more likely a person is to experience positive emotions such as pride, happiness, and satisfaction" (Turner & Stets, 2006, p. 32). Another generalization (from the power and status theories) has to do with formative career: "the more that individuals and collective actors hold power, prestige, and other resources or gain these resources, the more likely they are to experience such positive emotions as satisfaction, happiness, pride, well-being, and confidence" (Turner & Stets, 2006, p. 40). And, from exchange theory, the authors formulated a generalization (p. 46) pertaining to positive relationships: where people are mutually dependent on each other for resources, it is likely they will experience positive emotions in their relationship as well as express these feelings toward the other person or persons (e.g., in a triad). Furthermore Oatley, Keltner, and Jenkins (2006, pp. 221-222) present evidence for the proposition that the emotions expressed in a relationship, be they positive or negative, help shape the relationship.

Positive emotions may also influence the social atmosphere of groups, both large and small. For example Celia Ridgeway (1994) reported a study of the diverse emotions that may arise during group decision making. She observed that, when there is agreement in the group, positive emotion is likely to emerge, which in turn, tends to slant subsequent group decision making toward more agreement. This occurs, she holds, because positive emotions are more rewarding than negative ones, which tend to grow in a climate of disagreement.

Conclusion

Readers might ask, after having read this chapter, is there not more to personal development than what has been written here? The answer is yes, as the various textbooks in psychology bearing on personality formation, child development, and development over the lifespan amply demonstrate. But the present book is about sociology, not psychology. And, although there is important overlap between the two disciplines on the matter of personal development, it is sociology's distinctive contribution to our understanding of it as a positive process that is of interest here. I have argued in this chapter that this contribution can be framed in the language of formative career, favorable identity, attractive relationships, positive emotion, and several of their ancillary concepts.

Viewed from the perspective of positive sociology, personal development may be seen, in broad brushstrokes, as the foundation upon which the structure of self is built. In the next chapter we look at several positive building blocks that go into this structure, namely, self-efficacy, self-fulfillment, authenticity, well-being, and health. The self thus constructed, I argue there, is a confident self, a self who is its own agent and ready to pursue personally worthwhile activities.

Notes

1.   The idea of formative career, during which the person develops in significant measure, must be distinguished from non-formative career, wherein such development is largely, if not entirely, absent. Thus, many people have such careers in unskilled work, but movement through them can not be conceived of as personal development, but rather as something else such as accumulated earnings, years of service, or experience with different bosses.

2.   This discussion of education is, for all intents and purposes, about adult, or secondary, socialization. Here the learner, as agent, has a direct and active part in the learning process and in choosing what is to be learned. Not so with much of primary socialization, wherein learning centers the mandatory acquisition of the basic social and cultural precepts of the society. There is little personal agency here. Nonetheless such socialization is part of a complete positive sociology as an avenue for instilling certain social conditions (i.e., culture) in the individual.

3.   This excludes non-formative careers in simple, non-devotee small businesses such as residential rubbish collection, hotdog vending, and valet parking service.

5

The Confident Self

"There are admirable potentialities in every human being. Believe in your strength and your youth. Learn to repeat endlessly to yourself, 'It all depends on me.'"—André Gide

This is our main chapter on the confident self, the subject of which was broached in the preceding chapter. The confident self may be described, in terms commensurate with a positive sociology, as self-reliant and as inspiring people who are sure of themselves and their participation in those activities in which they are pursing a formative career. Furthermore the confident self, again seen from the angle of a positive sociology, consists of a substantial ability to understand both itself and the surrounding social and physical world. This includes an enhanced feeling of being able to solve, or at least affect in desirable ways, personal, communal, national, and, sometimes, even international problems, with work on the latter three nearly always achieved through some sort of collective action. The problems may be of the genre that so interest problem-centered sociologists, or they may be the positive problems and challenges that were briefly mentioned early in chapter 1, the ones to be met in the course of achieving or experiencing an OLL or OPL.

At the end of chapter 4, I likened the confident self to a structure. Self-efficacy is part of this structure; it gives direction to human agency in its quest for solutions to problems, both positive and negative. Other important components of this structure include self-fulfillment, authenticity, high quality of life and well-being, and decent health. Personal development is seen here as prerequisite to building personal confidence, even while this relationship is, to some extent, reciprocal. That is confidence in self certainly enhances movement through a formative career, in acquiring both formal and informal education and in establishing and maintaining positive relationships. And, lest we forget, I should like to reiterate that such development comes by way of serious leisure and devotee work. We turn now to the first of these building blocks, namely, self-efficacy.

Self-Efficacy

Psychologist Albert Bandura pioneered the concept of *self-efficacy*, defining it as "people's beliefs in their capabilities to produce desired effects by their own actions" (Bandura, 1997, p. vii). He argued that people develop "efficacy expectations" bearing on particular goals they hope to realize and on what they must do to achieve this. These expectations are based on the capabilities individuals believe they have to accomplish the goals they are pursuing in a particular setting. Bandura says that efficacy expectations constitute the cognitive state immediately preceding goal-directed actions. Additionally, efficacy is enhanced to the extent that people's *locus of control* is high; in other words they sense that the results of their activities are caused by themselves rather than by such impersonal forces as fate, luck, and chance (Rotter, 1990). Both concepts may be seen as constituents of human agency, as it operates during pursuit of positive goals.

If you think this description of self-efficacy reads much like the foregoing discussion of the confident self, you are right. The principal difference lies in the situational nature of the first compared with the trans-situational nature of the second. A person who feels confident about life as routinely led has, at least in part, built this view of self from numerous experiences of being efficacious in particular situations. In the language of positive sociology, confidence bubbles up from demonstrated self-efficacy in the core activities of a person's serious leisure and devotee work.

The main belief here is in one's own self-efficacy to pursue in a fulfilling way particular activities in serious leisure or devotee work. This belief in oneself is born of the numerous routine successes that accumulate with enduring, systematic pursuit of an activity and of the encouragement from positive others who also partake of it or who are otherwise close associates of the participant. Since confidence is closely aligned with self-efficacy, it is noteworthy that leisure educators strive to instil both in their clients and students. Datillo and Murphy (1991, pp. 147-152), for example, do this by encouraging participants in leisure to accept personal responsibility for their actions there. Leitner and Leitner (2004, pp. 313-314) first point out the need to overcome low self-esteem, then show how people may accomplish this through engaging in complex leisure.

Leisure educators also have a wealth of personal goals to suggest. Two of them are to strive for personal well-being and for a fine quality of life using pursuit of complex leisure as a means. A third goal is to try to turn pursuit of an activity in serious leisure or devotee work into a *central life interest*. Robert Dubin (1992) defines this interest as "that portion of a person's total life in which energies are invested in both physical/intellectual activities and in positive emotional states." Sociologically, a central life interest is commonly associated with a major role in life, such that the individual can rank its priority with reference to other major roles played there. In harmony with the preference in positive sociology for the idea of activity over that of role, we may say that it falls to leisure educators to urge their clients and students to seize on a serious leisure activity and make it a central life interest. Occupational counsellors might well promote these same goals with reference to the core activities of devotee work.

Self-efficacy is a central feature of positive psychology. Bandura says that here, however, the first should be seen as "coping self-efficacy." In this regard, he observed that "people avoid potentially threatening situations and activities, not because they are beset with anxiety, but because they believe they will be unable to cope with situations they regard as risky" (Bandura, 1989a, p. 1176). These people act to protect themselves, whatever their level of anxiety at the moment. The positive side of this emotional reaction is found in the parallel processes of control of anxiety arousal and avoidant behavior, both expressions of coping efficacy as perceived by the individual. In this way, people gain personal control over pervasive social threats.

Bandura is also aware of the influence of perceived coping efficacy on the basic biological systems that mediate health functioning. For instance stress has been identified as an important contributing condition to many physical dysfunctions. A person's capacity to control major events in life "appears to be a key organizing principle regarding the nature of these stress effects" (Bandura, 1989a, p. 1177). He says that exposure to physical stressors accompanied by a concomitant ability to control them generates no adverse physiological effects, whereas exposure to the same stressors with no ability to control them impairs the cellular components of the immune system. In a subsequent section we will consider some of the implications of health for the confident self.

Finally, bear in mind that mood and efficacy are reciprocally related, a proposition that brings negative emotion into the picture. We have, to this point, been considering only the positive influence of coping self-efficacy on emotion. Nevertheless Bandura's (e.g., 1989b) studies show that negative emotion can undermine feelings of efficacy, in contrast to positive emotion which can heighten those feelings. He also found that "the influence of induced mood on self-efficacy judgment is widely generalized across diverse domains of functioning" (Bandura, 1989b, p. 733).

Self-Fulfillment

Both as researchers on leisure and as participants in everyday life, we hear it all the time: "I sure had fun last night at the football game"; "It will be a fun time at Joan's sleep-over"; "it was a most enjoyable evening" (said to the host). Much less often do we hear leisure experiences being described as satisfying or fulfilling, even if, for their participants, some experiences have precisely that quality. Why these differences in choice of descriptors for positive leisure experience, and what do these four descriptors mean in science and common sense?

Commonsense usage of the four, as typical of common sense everywhere, is rather loose and for the first two broadly applied. Thus the adjective "fun" usually denotes finding pleasure or amusement in a particular activity, while the adjective "enjoyable" typically refers to an activity that can be enjoyed, that gives pleasure or delight. In other words, these two descriptors are basically synonyms. Turning to the third term, a satisfying experience, in one sense of the word, is itself synonymous with an experience that is fun or enjoyable (sometimes referred to as gratifying). But another sense of this adjective is substantially different: it refers to meeting or satisfying a need or want. Put otherwise a satisfying experience, in this second sense, leads to contentment with reference to a particular need or want, an additional meaning that sets it apart from the other three descriptors. By contrast, the fourth term, in one sense, points to a fulfilling experience, or more precisely, to a set of chronological experiences leading to development to the fullest of a person's gifts and character, to development of that person's full potential. A second sense of this adjective is, however, synonymous with the second sense of satisfying.

These four descriptors form a rough scale of depth of leisure experience, running from that which is superficial—fun—to that which is profound—fulfillment. In commonsense usage we seem, in crude fashion, to recognize these differences, in that, for example, few people would describe a sleep-over as fulfilling or a grueling marathon as fun or enjoyable. The task of leisure science, and this section, is to recognize the existence of this implicit, commonsense scale of leisure experience, while for scientific purposes, to try to iron out vagueness and inconsistency as these plague everyday usage of the four terms. We turn first to fun.

Because of the dual meaning of satisfaction, I have found it necessary, when striving to be as clear as possible about the rewards of serious leisure, to rely exclusively on the concept of fulfillment. It is substantially different from satisfaction, even in the second sense of the word. Serious leisure is about satisfying achievement and accomplishment, of that there is no doubt, but it is also about personal development and self-confidence, of maximizing one's gifts and character through pursuit of particular leisure activities (see Stebbins, 2004c). Meanwhile, satisfaction, I realized only a few years ago, can also mean, as noted in this section, becoming content or being content through gratification or pleasure experienced in an activity, which may well be of the casual leisure variety.

To avoid this confusion when talking about the rewards of serious leisure, it has become necessary to frame discussion in the less ambiguous language of fulfillment rather than the more ambiguous language of satisfaction. The latter is a slippery concept, primarily because it is cursed with two quite different meanings. Moreover, experiencing achievement (the second meaning) is not really the same as experiencing fulfillment. For the latter rests on a clear sense of a formative career (Stebbins, 2004c) in a complex role (found in work, leisure, a relationship, etc.), on the sense of realizing one's gifts and character over many years. Achievement, by contrast, results from a particular effort at a particular time in life. Thus fulfillment is, among several other things, a series of interrelated achievements interpreted by the achiever across a span of time.

Be that as it may, serious leisure enthusiasts do, at times, qualify their activities as fun. I have tried to deal with this seeming anomaly by invoking the idea of *gratification*. Over the years, I have come to describe as gratifying an activity that the participant sees as fun, but that also generates fulfillment. For instance, some of the kayakers in the Canadian Rockies whom I interviewed and who possessed the appropriate skills and experience said it is "fun" to paddle Class-4 Rivers. By this they meant that the activity is gratifying, because with time, they have acquired the technical qualifications to carry it off with relative ease (Stebbins, 2005b). This level of activity is fun, precisely because it is technically difficult but nonetheless quite manageable (it is fulfilling), given the participant's high level of development in the hobby.

In technical activities of this sort, fun has also been found to be a significant component of the flow experience, as seen in Csikszentmihalyi's

(1990, pp. 49, 72) linking of enjoyment with flow. But more recent thought on the matter by Seligman and Csikszentmihalyi (2000, p. 12) has led them to distinguish between the "pleasure" of what we have been calling fun (in casual leisure) from the "enjoyment" of activities referred to in this book as serious leisure. In this newer conceptualization enjoyment and self-fulfillment amount to the same thing.

Terms: Commonsense and Scientific

The popularity of the commonsense interpretation of the word fun as a way to describe leisure experiences at all levels of profundity shows the breadth of the problem facing leisure studies in this area. It follows that we must be careful when using this adjective in surveys, and be prepared in open-ended research procedures (e.g., semi-directed interviews, focus groups) to probe further to get the most precise understanding possible of its meaning for the respondent. The same holds for the plethora of commonsense adjectival synonyms for fun, including, enjoyable, pleasurable, agreeable, pleasing, amusing, diverting, entertaining, and interesting. And, although fewer synonyms have sprung up around the adjectives of satisfying and fulfilling, they do exist, and do contribute significantly to ambiguity in meaning there. In short, when employing such terms in research, we must never forget the subtle but far-reaching effects of popular usage.

The scientific definitions worked out in the preceding section, when contrasted with commonsense usage, may seem arbitrary, and to some extent they are precisely that. I have arbitrarily crafted definitions of satisfying and fulfilling intended to be mutually exclusive, that as near as I can tell have no overlap. I did the same thing many years ago when I believed it necessary to develop, from the mishmash of inconsistent and contradictory definitions found in the dictionaries of the day, a scientifically workable definition of "amateur" (Stebbins, 1979, pp. 21-22). Indeed, I have learned through experience that those sensitizing concepts which start life as commonsense ideas, if they are to perform their duties well, often require some provisional conceptual shaping (see also Van den Hoonaard, 1997, pp. 26-27).

What is important is that, as researchers, we be constantly aware of the popular tendency toward imprecise usage in this area of life, and try to fit that usage into a set of carefully worked out scientific definitions such as proposed here. I believe that the present set of concepts is not a Procrustean bed, however, for it allows for identification and analysis of the positive side of all leisure experiences, even while interview respondents sometimes use different terms. If we, as researchers, know both our scientific definitions and the context of the respondent's answers, we can, with minimal distortion, place those answers on the aforementioned scale. Or, in the case of surveys, we can word the questions and their fixed responses such that both reflect the scale and respondents are directed to tick the boxes describing well their leisure experiences.

Authenticity

Snyder and Lopez (2007, p. 241), who see authenticity as another aspect of positive psychology, define it as follows: "acknowledging and representing one's true self, values, beliefs, and behaviors to oneself and others." Stated otherwise being authentic means being honest with oneself and with one's presentation of self to others. Charles Taylor (1991, chap. 3) adds that being true to ourselves is a "powerful moral ideal." It is a form of personal sincerity. Still we must nuance Taylor's observation, by noting that our conception of authenticity is free of the connotation of moral correctness that is sometimes said to go with this trait. To be precise, some people are quite capable of being authentically deviant, of freely admitting, for example, that they are members of an aberrant religious group, patronize a local nudist resort, or light up the occasional marijuana joint. Tolerable deviance (Stebbins, 1996b), of which these three are instances, though morally wrong in the larger community, is generally not so strongly stigmatized there as to force into inauthentic silence those who practice certain varieties of it.

People seem to find forced inauthenticity constraining and therefore disagreeable. By the same token, they find, most attractive, those situations where they "can let their hair down" or "be themselves"; these give a positive face to their existence. In this regard, Silverberg (2008) learned, in a study of a Canadian energy company, that one of several reasons its employees gave for liking the firm was that they could be themselves. No posturing required in their work setting, quite unlike some others they had experienced.

In a positive sociology, authenticity comes to the confident self by way of personal development, specifically as achieved through positive interpersonal relationships and positive personal and social identity. Having achievements in work or leisure that the individual can be proud of and can therefore identify with, are, themselves, real and genuine features of that person's formative career. It follows that most people would like to see themselves in such terms (personal identity) and present themselves to, and be seen by, others in similar light (social identity). Such straightforward honesty also undergirds positive relationships, the more intimate of which commonly contain a window into the deeper reaches of each self in the bond.

Authenticity begets confidence through the mechanism of *realistic* assessment of self and relevant achievements. In part this happens when, using skill, knowledge, and experience, we compare ourselves with others pursuing the same activity. A kind of informal, personal ranking of self and those others is thereby reached, as reflected in the social mirror into which each individual looks to see how he or she is viewed by those others. The authentic person accepts this reflected social assessment as reasonably accurate. Thus a runner fond of participating in marathons who consistently places between the eightieth and ninetieth percentile of all contestants, if authentic, might say something on the order of "I am a good marathoner," but could not realistically say "I am a champion marathoner" (i.e., consistently placing among the top four participants in each race entered). Given this record other runners who know this one would tend to describe this person in similar terms.

Quality of Life and Well-Being

These two states were defined and discussed in chapter 3, but only as they bore on leisure. What remains to be done in the present section is to broaden this statement by relating the two to devotee work and the confident self. When we turn to quality of life and devotee work, it is evident that their relationship is the same as in serious leisure; all was in chapter 3 about quality of life in leisure applies equally to this kind of work. It, too, meets, in the same ways, the four components of quality of life.

High quality of occupational life, however generated, is a state of mind, which to the extent people are concerned with their own well-being at work, must as with serious leisure, be pursued with notable diligence. Moreover, high quality of working life does not magically appear. Rather it, too, roots in desire, planning, and patience, as well as in a capacity to seek and find satisfaction and fulfillment through experimentation with the core activities of the devotee's job. This leads eventually to what we discussed previously as an optimal positive lifestyle. Here, too, the watchword is agency. And occupational counsellors can advise and inform about work activities that hold strong potential for elevating quality of life on the job. Yet, in the end, it is the individual who must be motivated to pursue that quality and follow a plan for doing this, one possibly developed in collaboration with a counsellor.

Let us move on to well-being as it issues from occupational devotion. The conclusion here is that Warr's (1987) PEIs and Haworth's subsequent additions are similarly valid when applied to this kind of work as when applied to serious leisure. Moreover the exploratory hypothesis formulated in chapter 3 may now be expanded: that social well-being emanates from a high quality of life, as generated in a combination of serious leisure and devotee work balanced with casual leisure or project-based leisure, if not both. The empirical support for this assertion presented in chapter 3 came from the field of leisure studies, to which we may now join findings from research on what Florida (2002) has dubbed the "creative class." This set finds fulfillment at work though a variety of inventive core activities and in their free time in different serious leisure pursuits (pp. 169-170). But, alas, the same caveats apply, whether considering devotee work or serious leisure: research on the causal link between devotee work and well-being is only correlational, while such activity is, for some workers, capable of generating significant interpersonal and intrapersonal role conflict. Furthermore, the propensity toward selfishness is evident in this domain as well.

How do high quality of life and well-being, as gained through serious leisure and devotee work, relate to the confident self? My argument, which as far as I can tell has not been empirically assessed, is that feeling confident helps increase quality of life and subjective and social well-being. It joins with personal efficacy in the process of creating the benign and salubrious conditions that make our everyday lives worthwhile. This proposition is theoretically consistent with two of the four components of the want-based approach to quality of life: a sense of achievement in one's work (and I add leisure) and a sense of fulfillment of one's potential (in both work and leisure). That is, being confident helps boost a person's level of achievement and realize his native gifts and talents.

And how does the confident self relate to social well-being as Keyes (1998, p. 121) defined the latter: "the absence of negative conditions and feelings, the result of adjustment and adaptation to a hazardous world"? First, confidence in oneself is a positive feeling. Second, that confidence can aid adjustment and adaptation to the larger world, however hazardous the latter. The correlation of confidence with self-efficacy shows one mechanism for accomplishing this. Remember, as well, that confidence consists of a substantial ability to understand both oneself and the surrounding social and physical world. This includes an enhanced feeling of being able to solve, or at least affect in desirable ways, a range of problems. A sense of well-being is the result.

Health

Well-being includes having decent health, both mental and physical. Nevertheless these two states are so vital to life, in general, and self-confidence, in particular, that they beg to be treated of separately. To do otherwise is to risk losing them in the broader discussion of the other building blocks examined in this chapter. Another reason for giving special attention to health is the widespread tendency both in mainstream medical circles and among the general public to regard mental and physical health as largely, if not solely, a matter of diagnosis of, and treatment for, disease, injury, and debilitating bodily and mental development. Measures people and communities might take to prevent these problems are, in these two milieux, less often a concern. Yet, from the standpoint of a positive sociology, life for the most part, will seem much more agreeable when disease, injury, and debilitating developments are avoided, as opposed to having to live with them because the individual, the community, and the health care establishment, in some combination, failed to prevent them.

What have mental and physical health to do with the confident self? A great deal, I submit. For, to participate appropriately in many of the activities that are undertaken in the three domains of life, we must be confident of our capacity to do so at a personally and socially acceptable level. Furthermore, whether positive or negative, this participation rests on human agency, and this, in turn, depends on the health of the agent. For instance a woman who wants to paint her two-story house but worries she might fall off the ladder because she experiences occasional dizzy spells caused by an ear infection lacks confidence in her ability to meet this non-work obligation. A timpanist in a professional orchestra who has, the day of a concert, just learned his spouse has terminal cancer could understandably lose confidence in his ability to perform that evening. This possibility exists because he is unable to escape the thought of this upsetting turn of events. On the positive side a cross-country skier about to begin a race in what she believes is her best physical condition ever, is given, with this conviction, a boost in her confidence to compete well.

I get the impression that, in mainstream health circles, the term "leisure" is a dirty word. At least this sphere of life only seems to be discussed there largely, if not exclusively, in pejorative terms, I suspect because it is regarded, not as an avenue to the Heaven of good health, but as a road to the Hell of bad health. This commonsense view of leisure (i.e., casual leisure) in everyday life is, to be sure, partly valid. Some people do smoke, drink (alcohol), and eat too much, lead a sedentary existence when free of obligations, and watch television to the extent of dulling their wits, among many other sins of the flesh. Boredom in free time, though in fact not leisure, as was pointed out earlier, is nevertheless a further widely used indicator of the (mentally) unhealthy lifestyle that many a person fashions once work and other obligations are past.

But leisure is quite capable of generating healthy benefits. Although the relationship is surely more complex than this, we may say, in general terms, that self-fulfillment, whether experienced through serious leisure or project-based leisure (and we may add devotee work), leads to enhanced quality of life and well-being, and from there, to improved psychological health and physical health, to the extent the second is influenced by the first. So, even if the road to the Hell of bad health is paved, in part, with too steady and complete a diet of casual leisure, the one leading to the heaven of good health is paved, among other ways, with a judicious amount of serious leisure. We now know, however, that the pavement on the road to Heaven is composite; in light of the serious leisure perspective, we may say that it is also composed of some casual leisure or project-based leisure, if not both. And devotee work should be included as part of the composition of this route. In other words, to search for either an optimal leisure lifestyle or an optimal positive lifestyle is to get rolling along the road to good health.

All this, however, fits most logically within the framework of preventive medicine. Obviously, if a person already has bad or weak physical health, an optimal leisure or positive lifestyle is not, in itself, going to miraculously restore him to a healthy condition. Conceivably, someone with, say, bone cancer could still develop an optimal lifestyle of either type, which might in some way positively affect future mental health. In the meantime, however, that person is physically unhealthy and, so far as we know, neither work nor leisure, even when it includes significant physical exercise, can do anything to cure cancer. In other words, the proposition—fulfillment → quality of life → well-being → health—is most valid in the sphere of preventive health.

> The message, then, is prevention, not cure. And it is a message that needs to be heeded across the world as poor countries grow wealthier and adopt the eating habits and sedentary lives of the rich. It is an irony that evolution has shaped people to enjoy fat, sugar and indolence – things in short supply to man's hunter-gatherer ancestors, and desirable in the quantities then available. Wealth allows them to be indulged in abundance. Unfortunately, human bodies have evolved neither to cope, easily nor to resist. (*The Economist*, 2007, p. 94)

Unfortunately preventive medicine, as a profession, seems largely unaware of leisure's role in all this. In January 2005, I presented a seminar on it to the professors, research associates, and graduate students of the newly established Markin Institute at the University of Calgary. The Institute's mandate is to conduct research on and improve practice in preventive medicine and public health. My talk appeared to be warmly received, in good part, I should like to believe, because my ideas were seen as fresh. Few, if any, of those in attendance had thought of leisure as an avenue to the heaven of good health, though clearly, they knew of leisure's other road.

My little seminar has not transformed thinking in preventive medicine (even in Calgary, as near as I can tell), nor did I expect it would.[1] Here, as elsewhere in so much of modern life, the stereotype of leisure as pursuit of the trivial enjoys its own healthy existence. Here, as elsewhere, there is, as a result, great need for leisure education to spread knowledge about the entire serious leisure perspective. Life in free time can be much richer than the pleasures of hedonism. Nor should we forget devotee work when talking about preventive medicine. It is more difficult than serious leisure to find and sustain, but for those who manage to do this, their health should be enhanced.

Conclusion

Wilkins's (2001) study of a sample of elderly women with osteoporosis shows the functioning of the confident self. She classified twelve of her respondents as self-confident. She found that one source of their confidence lay in their sense of growth and mastery gained from previous life events, including divorce, which generated the assurance needed to master present and subsequent events in life. These women balanced their everyday existence through participation in valued activities, while making plans for the future. Work, volunteering, non-work obligations, and other complex activities gave them meaning. Wilkins (2001, pp, 81-82) wrote that

> Their views of the self were as a competent partner, mother, friend, worker or volunteer, as healthy and as independent. Those with confident selves drew on and benefitted from support from others. They sought social approval and validation of their extant selves through interactions with others. Feedback from others confirmed their self-pictures (reflected appraisals).

The women scored high on measures of self-acceptance, environmental mastery, and purpose in life. Thus Wilkins's study illustrates the confident self in action. It shows substantial ability among the twelve respondents to understand both themselves and their surrounding social and physical world. For them an enhanced feeling emerged from being able to solve, or at least affect in desirable ways, key personal problems. The result was a more attractive lifestyle than they would have had were they lacking self-confidence.

In some scholarly circles all this would be subsumed under the rubric of gerontological "resilience" (e.g., DeMuth, 2004). Still resilience is not necessarily predicated on confidence; hence it would be inaccurate to regard the two as equivalent ideas. We may still hypothesize, however, that, other conditions equal, resilience is more effective when inspired by a confident self than when it is not.

The underlying model here is that the confident self takes root in individuals, where confidence is constructed from the various building blocks described in this chapter. Sociology stresses the social interactive nature of this personal development, while acknowledging the important contribution made by psychology to explaining it in other ways. In fact the present chapter shows better than any of the others in this book the articulation of positive psychology and sociology. Yet nearly everyone, confident or not, lives in a larger sociopolitical world of, these days, extraordinary complexity. Being confident in and realistically attuned to their relevant abilities, aids immensely their quest to solve the problems they meet in this world, be they personal, or those that may be qualified as communal, national and, at times, even international. True the latter three are nearly always managed through collective action of some sort, where individuals meet and collaborate with others who themselves possess varying degrees of self-confidence. And the problems faced may be of the kind that interest problem-centered sociology, or they may be the problems and challenges people confront while trying to achieve or experience an attractive lifestyle.

The next chapter bears on this larger world, a chapter that is therefore substantially more sociological than the present one. Chapter 6 shows off better than this chapter the essential features of a positive sociology. Since Durkheim sociology has always been distinguished by its central interest in the *sui generis* nature of social phenomena. That is collective entities such as groups, organizations, communities, and whole societies are assumed to have a unique and identifiable character of their own. They are entities in themselves, not reducible to their component parts, to their individual members. In other words, in sociology at least, the social whole has always been assumed to be greater than the sum of its parts. A positive sociology stresses the personally attractive aspects of these unique, abstract entities, as we have already seen in elementary form, in the treatment of interpersonal relationships presented earlier in the present chapter. The banner that a positive sociology should fly at this level is community involvement and its progeny, social capital.

Note

1.   A year or so after my talk to the Markin Institute, a draft of its organizational plan turned up in my e-mail box. On page 9 "recreation" and "neighborhood sporting clubs" appear in the list of mechanisms leading to good health. These are not my words, but just the same, they are welcome signs that, in the eyes of researchers at this Institute, leisure does figure in the formula for mental and, possibly, physical well-being.

6

Community Involvement

"Community involvement" has become, for many people, one of those warm and fuzzy ideas that send shivers of virtue, kindliness, and compassion up and down the spine. Not surprising, since a similar sentimental *frisson* is also felt in the same circles when the word "community" enters the conversation. Both concepts, in the least discerning of conceptualizations, constitute an unalloyed good. Both are, from this point of view, wholly positive.

This chapter, too, concentrates on the positive, as it should in a disquisition on positive sociology. But the following definition of community involvement is neutral enough to also admit consideration of its negative elements, thereby enabling us to achieve a more balanced understanding of the process than delivered by its more popular image as pure goodness:

> Community involvement is local voluntary action, where members of a local community participate together in nonprofit groups or in other community activities. Often the goal here is to improve community life. This concept, which is synonymous with those of civic, civil, citizen, and grassroots involvement, is broader than that of "citizen participation," in that it includes both local political voluntary action and nonpolitical voluntary action. (Smith, Stebbins & Dover, 2006, p. 52)

According to this definition, the goal is often to improve communal life. Often, yes, but not invariably. For, as will become apparent shortly, a number of leisure activities do not have as their goal such improvement, even if, at times, some of them effect it anyway.

In this chapter, I consider the potential that especially serious and project-based leisure have for generating social capital through community involvement. To understand this potential, we must examine the myriad organizational ties that have their origin in leisure (running from dyads through groups to social movements). We must also discuss the nonprofit sector, altruism, and volunteering as leisure, as the latter is manifested in serious, casual, and project-based form. Next, as a continuation of chapter 4, we look into the communal ramifications of the Internet. Then I tackle the tendency toward selfishness, drawing on Charles Taylor's position on this attitude and its relationship to the authentic self. Selfishness is related to certain the values and moral standards germane to community involvement. The chapter ends with a section on care and community involvement. Occupational devotion is, by and large, omitted from all this, since work, defined here as coerced (non-voluntary) activity, cannot be a source of community involvement as just defined.

First, however, since our definition of community involvement rests, in part, on the process of voluntary action, we must look at it and how it fits with leisure.

Leisure and Voluntary Action

Smith, Stebbins, and Dover (2006, pp. 237-238) define "voluntary action" as:

> action by individuals or nonprofit groups stemming from voluntary altruism. In voluntary action individuals, alone or in groups, reach beyond their own personal, often selfish, interests to act in harmony with a combination of the following: service, citizenship, socio-religious values and other values. In their broadest sense such beliefs motivate people to act as if others in their society mattered, an outgrowth of certain cultural and subcultural values of a nation.

According to Smith (2000, pp. 19-20) altruism is voluntary when there is (1) a mix of humane caring and sharing of oneself and one's resources; (2) at least a moderate freedom to chose the activity; (3) a lack of coercion from biophysical, biosocial, or socially compelling forces; (4) a sensitivity to certain needs and wants of a target of benefits; (5) an expectation of little or no remuneration or payment in kind; and (6) an expectation of receiving some sort of satisfaction for action undertaken on behalf of the target. Moreover voluntary action includes quasi-volunteering, while to the extent it is based strictly on hedonic self-interest, it excludes most types of casual leisure. The exception here is, of course, casual volunteering. Smith (2000, pp. 25, 47) defines "quasi-volunteer" as one who receives a stipend that is significantly less than market value of the labor provided (e.g., Peace Corps volunteers).

What, then, is the relationship between voluntary action and voluntary altruism, on the one hand, and leisure, on the other? This relationship is paramount for this book, since I have been arguing from the start that leisure is a wellspring for positive sociology. Though much of modern leisure can be considered part of the nonprofit sector, free-time activities not motivated by voluntary altruism, including most individual casual leisure (e.g., napping, strolling, daydreaming, hot-tubbing), lie outside that sector. Individual casual leisure is hedonically self-motivated. Thus voluntary action is typically a leisure activity, especially the contributions of the pure volunteer, who receives no remuneration whatsoever and no reimbursement for out-of-pocket expenses (Smith, 2000, p. 24).

The interrelationship of voluntary action, voluntary altruism, and leisure are well illustrated in the activities of the mentor. Although some mentors are organized and carry out their work within a formal organization, a good deal of mentoring, indeed possibly most of it, takes place elsewhere, on an informal plane. Formally or informally, a mentor is someone who, with regard to a particular area of life, is both trusted and respected by a protégé, where trust and respect are based on a significant level of experience and knowledge that the latter believes the former to possess. Superiority in this regard is critical, for why would the protégé accept an equal or an inferior in this role when superior experience and knowledge are what the protégé seeks. Mentoring, in this conceptualization, is understood as volunteer activity, as small-scale altruism (Stebbins, 2006c).

Community Involvement as Leisure

Much of what I have written in the past under this heading has borne on the contributions made by serious leisure enthusiasts to the social and cultural enrichment of their local community. This kind of community involvement is evident when, for example, the town's civic orchestra provides it every three or four months with a concert of classical music or the local astronomy society offers an annual "star night" during which the public may observe the heavens using the telescopes of club members. And model railroaders in the area sometimes mount for popular consumption exhibitions of the fruits of their hobby. Lyons and Dionigi (2007) found, in a study of older Australian adults in Masters sports, that, through their participation there, they feel a sense of "giving something back" to the community. Though most thinkers in the area fail to conceive of these activities as voluntary action, they certainly fit the definition of such action, as do the activities discussed in the next paragraph. Furthermore Hemmingway (1999) and Reid (1995) have argued that, when considering leisure's contribution to community, it is important to distinguish between different kinds of activities. The examples above—all of them serious leisure—illustrate contributions quite distinct from those made through casual or project-based forms.

A broader sort of community involvement (sometimes also carried out on a regional or societal level) comes from pursuing volunteer activities, which may be enacted as serious, casual, or project-based leisure. This is the most common conception of "community involvement," which is often discussed as "civil labor." It, too, is voluntary action, although a type that finds members of a local community participating together as volunteers in nonprofit groups or other community activities. On this level, a principal intention is to improve community life. Civil labor, which is broadly synonymous with community involvement, differs mainly in emphasis; it is on human activity devoted to unpaid renewal and expansion of social capital (Rojek, 2002, p. 21). Beck (2000, p.125) says that civil labor comprises housework, family work, club work, and volunteer work. This is an extremely general conception, however, since it includes the area of unpaid work, the domain of non-work obligation.

Rojek (2002, pp. 26-27) argues that, for the most part, civil labor consists of the community contribution made by amateurs, hobbyists, and career volunteers when they pursue their serious leisure. This is precisely what Leadbeater and Miller (2004) have in mind in their book about how amateurs in various fields are shaping the twenty-first-century economy and society in the West. Helft (2007) offers a concrete example in an article about amateur mapmakers, who using simple Internet tools, are reshaping online map services and offering viewers far more detail of many more geographic sites than heretofore.[1] Along these same lines Levine (2007) holds that democracy depends on citizen participation and that too many of today's young Americans lack the skills needed for this.

Civil labor, however conceived of, generates "social capital," defined here, following Putnam (2000, p. 19), as the links among individuals manifested in social networks, trustworthiness, acts motivated by the norm of reciprocity, and the like that develop in a community or larger society. The term is an analogy to the concepts of human capital and physical capital (e.g., financial resources, natural resources); it emphasizes that human groups of all kinds also benefit from and advance their interests according to the salutary interrelations of their members. Community involvement also generates social capital, but as noted earlier, it includes amateur and hobbyist activities, where this result, though it occurs, is not their primary purpose.

With one exception to be discussed in the next paragraph, casual leisure appears not to make this kind of contribution to community. True, people are sometimes joined in such leisure with strangers, especially these days, over the Internet. The same happens with *tribes*: fragmented groupings left over from the preceding era of mass consumption, groupings recognized today by their unique tastes, lifestyles, and form of social organization (Maffesoli, 1996). Maffesoli identifies and describes this postmodern phenomenon, which spans national borders. In this regard, he observes that mass culture has disintegrated, leaving in its wake a diversity of tribes, including the followers of heavy metal music and those youth who participate in raves. Tribes are special leisure organizations, special ways of organizing the pursuit of particular kinds of casual leisure. Tribes are also found in serious leisure, but not, however, in project-based leisure (see Stebbins, 2002, pp. 69-71). Tribes, social worlds, casual leisure, and serious leisure are related in Figure 6.1.

Figure 6.1
Structural Complexity: From Tribes to Social Worlds

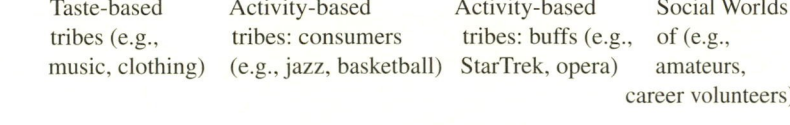

| Taste-based tribes (e.g., music, clothing) | Activity-based tribes: consumers (e.g., jazz, basketball) | Activity-based tribes: buffs (e.g., StarTrek, opera) | Social Worlds of (e.g., amateurs, career volunteers) |

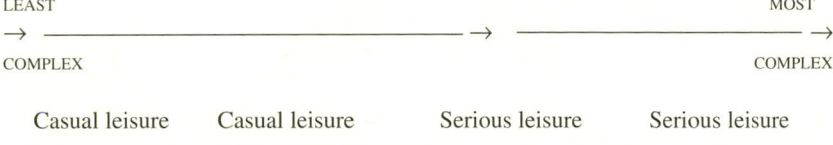

LEAST			MOST
→ ————————————	→	————————————	→
COMPLEX			COMPLEX

| Casual leisure | Casual leisure | Serious leisure | Serious leisure |

From: Stebbins, R.A. (2002. *The organizational basis of leisure participation: A motivational exploration.* State College, PA: Venture, p. 70.)

But, in the taste- and activity-based tribal casual leisure just mentioned, scant contribution is made to the community. I have also excluded from this discussion of community involvement the type of casual leisure observed in regular sessions of sociable conversation among friends or acquaintances, for example, in the *kaffeeklatsch*, with the gang at the pub, and during the friendly gathering after weekly religious services. To be sure, they are both social and voluntary, but they are not, however, altruistic voluntary action. It follows that they are neither civil labor nor generators of social capital. Hence they cannot be qualified as civil labor.

This, as already noted, is also true of nearly all other casual leisure, the glaring exception being, of course, casual volunteering; it is done expressly as civil labor. And, in the course of doing it, volunteers may well meet and serve with people never before encountered. So we must conclude, contrary to Rojek, that such labor is not limited to serious leisure, but also finds its place in the volunteer type of casual leisure.

Moreover volunteer project-based leisure may be conceived of as civil labor. Project-based leisure has potential in at least two ways for building community. First, it too can bring into contact people who otherwise have no reason to meet, or at least meet frequently. Second, by way of event volunteering and other short-term, collective altruistic activity, it can contribute to carrying off community events and projects. In other words some project-based leisure (mostly one-shot volunteer projects, it appears) can also be conceived of as civil labor, as just defined, suggesting that such activity may be other than serious leisure. In fact, the mountain hobbyists studied by the author (Stebbins, 2005b) occasionally rounded out their leisure lifestyles by sporadically undertaking or participating in (typically volunteer) projects of this nature.

Clearly, to be community involvement, leisure must be collective in some fashion; the reclusive hobbies (e.g., liberal arts, some amateur piano and guitar), for example, fail to qualify. Furthermore, when it comes to social capital, as opposed to civil labor and community involvement, I do not believe a case exists for privileging any of the three forms of leisure as the principal or most important way of generating the former. What is important is that people come together in voluntary action, as motivated by voluntary altruism, doing so long enough to learn something about one another, learn to trust one another (where experience warrants), develop "other-regarding" or altruistic love for one another (Jeffries et al., 2006), and for these reasons become willing to continue their interaction. True, many forms of serious leisure encourage sustained contact capable of fostering such learning, as seen in routine participation in many volunteer emergency services, hobbyist clubs, and arts and sports groups. Project leisure can also be a source of social capital, though here, such capital is of more limited scope than that generated through enduring serious leisure activities. As for casual leisure volunteering, it may be short term or long term.

Leisure and Organization

In leisure, as in most other areas of life, many activities are structured, or organized, in small groups, social networks, and grassroots organizations as well as in larger complex organizations and still more broadly, in tribes (considered in the previous section), social worlds, and social movements (Stebbins, 2002). Each structures the social behavior of its members in particular ways, some of those ways being unique to that kind of organization. And, as stated earlier, individual interests also structure the organizational entities that facilitate these interests, which includes establishing those entities in the first place. Here the positive role of human agency is again evident. Thus we may say about leisure organizations, as with other kinds of organizations, that participation in them amounts to a two-way street of influence running from individual to collectivity and the reverse. This is the first of three critical assumptions on which this discussion of leisure and organization is based.

The second critical assumption is that members of the different sorts of organizations (defined below in the wide sense of social organization) know they are members. Third, such people value highly their membership, for given that we are considering only leisure organizations entered without coercion, members would abandon them were they substantially disvalued. Moreover, when they are highly valued, belonging itself becomes an important motive, since membership enables pursuit of one or more of the leisure activities the organization promotes and facilitates and its members are eager to pursue. Yet it should be clear that belonging to any of these organizational entities, even when centered on leisure, is never wholly a positive experience; for example, spouses have their tiffs, dissension shakes up some groups, ideological tensions can splinter a social movement, and so on.

Let us note before going further into the matter of the organization of leisure that many leisure activities in all three forms also appear to allow for, if not require, solitary participation, volunteering being the chief exception. Thus, someone may, in solitude, play the piano or the guitar, collect rocks or seashells, sit and daydream, or assemble a complicated electronic device from a kit. Volunteering, however, is inherently organizational in the broad sense of the word, since by definition, it involves directly or indirectly serving other people, be they individuals or groups. What, then, do I mean by "the broad sense" of the concept of organization?

"Organization" is used here as shorthand for the range of collectivities mentioned at the start of this section (dyads to social movements) that add social and psychological structure to leisure life. Accordingly, discussion in this section will center primarily on these different types manifested as leisure organizations rather than on the community or societal organization of leisure, as seen in the sweeping communal arrangements that make available leisure services and opportunities. Additionally the present book requires presentation of only an *aperçu* of the different kinds of organization common in leisure, with a fuller treatment of them being available elsewhere (Stebbins, 2002).

So, in harmony with what was said in chapter 4 about positive relationships, note that some leisure is pursued in dyads (e.g., two friends organizing a surprise birthday party for someone or going together to the cinema). The triad is also a recognizable arrangement within which to partake of leisure (e.g., three people on a fishing trip, a classical music trio), and the same holds for the small group (e.g., church basketball team, several friends who routinely hike together, four couples who dine monthly at a restaurant). These three types of organization are found in all three forms of leisure.

Turning to social network the definition that best fits the small amount of work done on this form of organization within the domain of leisure is Elizabeth Bott's (1957, p. 59). Hers is simple: a *social network* is "a set of social relationships for which there is no common boundary." In the strict sense of the word, a network is not a structure, since it has no shared boundaries (boundaries recognized by everyone in the structure), no commonly recognized hierarchy, and no central coordinating agency. Nevertheless, links exist between others in the network, in that some members are directly in touch with each other while other members are not.

As individuals pursue their leisure interests, they commonly develop networks of friends and acquaintances related in one way or another to these interests. When a person acquires more such interests, the number of networks tends to grow accordingly, bearing in mind, however, that members of some of these will sometimes overlap. For instance, a few members of John's dog breeding network—they might be suppliers, veterinarians, or other breeders—are also members of his golf network—who might be suppliers, course personnel, or other golfers. Knowing about people's leisure networks helps explain how they, through positive agency, socially organize their leisure time. In this manner, as Blackshaw and Long (1998, p. 246) pointed out, we learn something new about leisure lifestyle.

At the next level of organization – the grassroots association – serious leisure predominates, though some manifestations of it can also be found in casual leisure. The very nature of project-based leisure would seem to preclude grassroots associations from developing in this form. According to Smith (2000, p. 8):

> grassroots associations are locally based, significantly autonomous, volunteer-run formal nonprofit (i.e., voluntary) groups that manifest substantial voluntary altru-

ism as groups and use the associational form of organization and, thus, have official memberships of volunteers who perform most, and often all, of the work/activity done in and by these nonprofits.

The term "formal" in this definition refers in fact to a scale of structure and operations that, in an actual association, may be informal, semiformal, or formal. Moreover, the line separating grassroots associations from paid-staff voluntary groups—treated of in the next paragraph as volunteer organizations—is unavoidably fuzzy, distinguishing the two being primarily a matter of gradation. Both types fall under the heading of *voluntary groups*: "nonprofit groups of any type, whether grassroots associations or based on paid staff, and whether local, national, or international in scope" (Smith, 2000, p. ix). In harmony with this statement we may say that all the groups listed in the preceding paragraph are also grassroots associations, as are such formal entities as Girl Guide troops, stamp collectors' societies, singles' clubs, outlaw biker gangs, and college fraternities and sororities.

By comparison, volunteer organizations offer leisure only to career and casual volunteers and to volunteers serving on projects. Volunteer organizations are distinguished by their reliance on paid staff, and by the fact that they are established to facilitate work for a cause or provision of a service rather than pursuit of a pastime. They nonetheless depend significantly on volunteer help to reach their objectives.

Pearce (1993, p. 15) holds that by far the largest number of volunteers work in these organizations. Yet some volunteer organizations may be staffed entirely by remunerated employees, volunteers only being engaged as unpaid members of their boards of directors. Hospitals and universities present two main examples. Many foundations can be similarly classified. Other volunteer organizations have a more even mix of paid and volunteer personnel; they include Greenpeace, Amnesty International, and the Red Cross. Finally, some have only one or two employees, with all other work being conducted by volunteers. They are, at bottom, grassroots associations that have grown complicated enough to justify paying someone to help with certain of the group's routine operations that its volunteers are unable or unwilling to carry out.

Leisure service organizations are not voluntary groups, as just defined. Rather, they are collectivities consisting of a paid staff who provide one of more leisure services to a targeted clientele. To be sure, the clients are engaging in particular leisure activities, but the organizations providing them are not themselves leisure organizations of the sort considered in this section. Leisure service organizations are established either to make a profit, the goal of many a health spa, amusement park, and bowling center, for example, or in some instances, to simply make enough money to continue offering their services. This is the goal of charitable, nonprofit groups like Meals on Wheels, the YMCA and YWCA, and the Elderhostel Programs as well as governmental leisure and recreational programs and services.

The next two types of organization germane to leisure have already been considered; social worlds were described in chapter 1 and tribes were covered earlier in this chapter. Let me now add that the richest development of social worlds may be observed in serious leisure, and if found at all in casual and project-based leisure, they are, by comparison, much simpler in composition. Refer to figure 6.1 for a schematic view of the interrelationship of these two types of organization with casual and serious leisure.

What remains, then, to be examined in this section on leisure and organization is the social movement. A *social movement* is a non-institutionalized set of networks, small groups, and formal organizations that has coalesced around a significant value, which inspires members to promote or resist change with reference to it. The first question is whether participation in a social movement is a leisure activity. The answer is both yes and no, for it depends on the movement in question. Movements abound that gain members through their own volition, suggesting that the members experience no significant coercion to become involved. Some religious movements serve as examples, as do movements centered on values like physical fitness and healthy eating. Still, the latter two also include people who feel pressured by outside forces to participate, as when their physician prescribes exercise and weight loss or face an early death. Thus some social movements are composed of enthusiasts who are there for leisure reasons and other people who are compelled to be there (not leisure). Finally, there are movements that seem to find their impetus primarily in people who feel driven to champion a particular cause, such as the celebrated temperance movement of early last century and the vigorous antismoking movement of modern times. A strong sense of obligation fuels participation in them. Those who make up the gun control and nuclear disarmament movements seem cut from the same cloth. Whether this is leisure must be determined empirically through direct research on the motivation of members.

Social movements, be they primarily of the leisure variety, the forced variety, or a combination of the two, have left a prominent mark on modern and postmodern life. Homer-Dixon (2007), for instance, commenting on the success of the mothers' movement in the 1960s that championed banning atmospheric nuclear testing, a practice that contaminated children's milk, now urges a similar formation fired by the goal of trying to bring global warming under control. Thus, considered alone, a social movement is a distinctive form of organization, which provides serious and casual leisure for volunteers. Further they are also likely to provide leisure projects for volunteers, enabling the latter to become involved for a limited period of time with a movement. Examples include participating in a fund-raising campaign, organizing a major rally, or lobbying for a crucial piece of legislation.

All the kinds of organization considered in this section relate to formative career and life course as described in chapter 3, for they act as links for people through their various leisure roles and activities to associated statuses and community organizational structures. Consider two cases. One is a man serving (activity/role) as member of the board of directors of a local arts council (director as status in a volunteer organization) also has an identifiable place in his community. It is likewise for a woman coaching (activity/role) an amateur basketball team (coach as status in an amateur group). Both participants, in pursuing their leisure careers this way, simultaneously find a respectable and recognizable place in the larger community, which I have argued elsewhere (Stebbins, 2002, pp. 34-35) is a motivational reward of its own. Organization also influences the life course, which is exemplified in such long-term role intersections as the volunteer policies of an individual's employer (work-role influence) and the demands made on that person by family (family-role influence).

The Internet

We explored the Internet in chapter 4, treating of it there as a main, modern-day source of information and knowledge. In the present chapter I inquire into how it facilitates diverse, distinctive manifestations of leisure organization and community involvement, and how it has acquired enormous significance in many segments of the contemporary population. Today these manifestations, when they function as favorable forces in the community, are as important as any we have looked at so far in this treatise on positive sociology. In this regard, the Internet and its communal ramifications amount to an extremely complex and far-reaching subject, which I will by no means fully examine in this book. My object in this section is far more modest; it is simply to present a sample of ways the Web fosters community involvement.

The earliest online gathering of a group of people occurred over AR-PANET, where in a demonstration in1972, a number of academics writing from different computers exchanged messages about the possible uses of this invention on the World Wide Web (www.isoc.org/history, retrieved 19 September 2007). It was primarily academics who used ARPANET and other networks, until development in the early 1980s of public counterparts, most notably, BITNET and USENET. The "newsgroup," where numerous users in different locations would send messages to others in the group and which operated through USENET, was one of the prominent early networks.

The newsgroup was but one of many Internet Forums, which went by various names, among them "message board," "discussion board," "bulletin board," and "discussion group." Each was designed for holding discussions and receiving content from users, each was, so to speak, an electronically interactive bulletin board. Sometimes this content and ensuing discussion was general and community wide, sometimes it was more narrowly limited to a particular subject and a select set of participants. Messages were received chronologically, often generating interactive commentary forming a "thread," or chain, of remarks made over time by all active users.

The newsgroups disseminated factual messages, or at least the messages were intended to be factual, if not newsworthy. The "chat room," by contrast, was more unabashedly about mood, opinion, attitude, and so on. It, too, was a mode of communication within a group (small or large), accomplished by sending typed ("text") messages to all the people who had joined a particular chat room. Talk in these rooms could be about nearly anything, providing the group wanted to discuss it, though usually, the room was established by one or more members for the purpose of discussing certain matters presumed to be of interest to a target clientele. For instance, a leisure-oriented room might be set up to talk about a particular soap opera or sports team. Chat room talk was not necessarily a leisure activity, however, in that they also sprang up in certain occupations where information and opinion of a professional nature could be shared. They may have been modeled on the older "chatline," which is a telephone service facilitating conversation among a number of people each on separate lines. Newsgroups and chat rooms still operate today, but their popularity has been usurped by newer developments.

The "blog" is of much more recent origin, the term being a portmanteau of "web log." It is a website, where entries are received in chronological order (usually the most recent appearing at the head of the list). Some blogs invite information or commentary on a subject, say, a political issue or a social problem. Others are essentially personal diaries. All blogs are interactive, in that "bloggers" respond with their own understanding of and reaction to what one or more people have written earlier. Much of what appears in the millions of blogs on the Web today is textual, but photos, videos, music, and other material are also added from time to time. From the standpoint of leisure organization, an interactive blog resembles most closely a social network.

"Facebook" was founded in 2004. Its website (www.facebook.com, retrieved 18 September 2007) describes it as "a social utility that connects you with the people around you." Everyone is invited to subscribe to it. Through it subscribers may upload photos or publish notes about themselves. Here they may receive news from friends, post videos, organize a search for a missing person, and almost any number of other conceivable uses. Privacy settings are available to control who sees what people post in their own facebooks. It is also possible to join networks composed of some of the people who live, study, or work around you. In leisure terminology, Facebook may serve a group or a social network. "MySpace," a similar social networking service founded in 2006, is now rivaling Facebook. "YouTube," which was inaugurated in 2005, is similar to these two only in the sense that it features video clips posted by individuals for users throughout the cyberworld to view. YouTube also features some blogs centered on the videos posted there. All this is part of the era of Web 2.0, of community-building tools, peer-to-peer networking, and the open source movement.

These three, many of the blogs, and some of the other electronic social networks are operated by third parties, for whom a main interest is establishing and running them. Additionally people with the necessary technical knowledge coupled with an interest they wish to promote may develop their own web pages either for a select clientele or for literally all in cyber space. This, too, is a kind of community involvement.

Facebook, MySpace, and the blogs seem especially vulnerable to becoming vehicles for, among other practices, defamation, falsehoods, impersonations, malicious gossip, and identity fraud, clear proof that these forms of leisure organization have both a positive and a negative communal side. The three also facilitate "cyberbullying," or bullying someone over the Internet, usually a particular child or adolescent. Bullies have even been known to establish web pages for this purpose, though they risk discovery since such pages must have a traceable source. Moreover, web pages may be established for deviant purposes (e.g., swinging, nudism, deviant religion). All these examples meet the criteria of community involvement contained in the definitions presented earlier in this chapter, definitions which make no claim that such involvement need only be of the conventional, nondeviant variety.

The various forums operated on a dial-up basis during the 1980s and 1990s. Then, in the later 1990s, the Web-based forums just mentioned began to appear. A sense of being a member of a special group often developed around forums sustained by regular users, this constituting one of their positive sociological features. As in the chat rooms the subject of discussion could be about nearly anything (work, leisure, obligation), one main challenge being to find a sufficient number of people willing to participate over the long term.

Thanks to the advent of broadband Internet connections, the personal computer game has now become socially organized, in the sense that individual players can compete against others across the vast range of the Internet. Before, this gaming was confined to people playing against each in other Local Area Networks (LANs), who were limited by the weak connections of the dial-up services at that time. Now many more players can join a game, doing so from any place in the world served by broadband.

In fact, the popularity of these games has grown, commensurate with the ease that players can now enter the online competition. Affordable, widespread high-bandwidth Internet connections enable large numbers of players to interact with each other within the framework of a given game, giving rise to the phenomenon of the "massively multiplayer online role-playing games" (MMORPGs). Nonetheless it is still possible to participate in online computer games using dial-up modems, even though most participants consider the broadband Internet connection necessary as a means for reducing the "gap" in time separating player responses.

From the angle of a positive sociology, the online computer game facilitates a distinctive sort of agreeable social interaction among people who, apart from the game, are typically strangers to one another. It is, however, but a facsimile of the kind of agreeable interaction examined in chapter 5, as experienced in a positive quality of life realized, in part, through sociable conversation and plenty of opportunities for face-to-face interpersonal contact. Nonetheless Luft (2007) found that gamers have met other gamers online, established lasting friendships, at times even marital relationships, which got their start in, for example, a MMORPG. Although she observed that such games may be played alone, they are most commonly played over the Internet with other people.

Widespread use of the Internet also has certain far-reaching social consequences, James Slevin (2007) has observed. For instance it de-traditionalizes modern social life, among other ways, by facilitating horizontal communication that undermines authority, which tends to run vertically. Slevin also lists several "challenges" posed by the Internet, all of which may be conceived of as bearing on community involvement:

> First, to what extent is the Internet facilitating an advance in intelligent relationships between individuals, groups, and organizations arranged through dialogue rather than domination and violence? Second, how might the Internet empower individuals, groups, and organizations to make things happen rather than have things happen to them in the context of overall goals and interests? Third, in what way does the Internet offer a new basis for solidarity and strategic alliances, bringing together in association individuals, groups, and organization who were previously socially and geographically far apart? Fourth, in what way might the Internet open up new opportunities for limiting damage and conflict as new communication networks allow individual, groups, and organizations to cross paths with each other whose views differ from their own? (p. 2385)

These challenges will test, in both negative and positive ways, social life in all three domains of our existence, certainly including that segment of it referred to here as community involvement.

Selfishness

It would be reasonable to ask why a section on something as negative as selfishness appears in a book bearing on the positive side of human social life? The answer is, in part, that I promised to present a balanced picture of the warm and fuzzy idea of community involvement. Selfishness is in one sense negative, especially for the people who are victims of it, but viewed through the lens of community involvement it may also have certain positive consequences.

Selfishness is the act of a self-seeker judged as selfish by the victim of that act (Stebbins, 1981). When we define an act as selfish, we make an imputation. This imputation is most commonly hurled at perceived self-seekers by their victims, where the self-seekers are felt to demonstrate a concern for their own welfare or advantage at the expense of or in disregard for those victims. The central thread running through the fabric of selfishness is exploitative unfairness—a kind of personal favoritism infecting the everyday affairs of may people in modern society. In comparing the three forms, it is evident that serious leisure is nearly always the most complicated and enduring of them and, for this reason, often takes up much more of a participant's time (Stebbins, 1995). It is therefore much more likely to generate charges of selfishness. For instance some types of serious, and even some project-based, leisure can only be pursued according to a rigid schedule (e.g., amateur theatrical rehearsals, volunteer guide work at a zoo, volunteer ticket selling at an arts festival), which unlike most casual leisure, allows little room for compromise or manoeuvre. Thus imputations of selfishness are considerably more likely to arise with regard to the first two.

Furthermore we can make a similar observation about serious and causal leisure activities that exclude the participant's partner vis-à-vis those that include this person. Logically speaking, it is difficult to complain about someone's selfishness when the would-be complainer also engages in the activity, especially with significant fulfillment. Furthermore serious leisure, compared with casual leisure, is often more debatable as selfishness, when seen from the standpoints of both the victim and the self-seeker. For serious leisure enthusiasts have at their fingertips as justifications for their actions such venerated ideals as self-enrichment, self-expression, self-actualization, service to others, contribution to group effort, development of a valued personal identity, and the regeneration of oneself after work. As for casual volunteering it is a partial exception to this observation, in that it, too, can be justified by some of these ideals, most notably volunteer service to others and regeneration.

I have argued elsewhere (Stebbins, 2006a, p. 75) that selfishness is part of the culture of leisure, a proposition based on my observations over the years that many participants in all three forms share a tendency to act in this way. Moreover this tendency and the problems it can engender appear to be fully recognized in leisure circles, though admittedly, the matter has yet to be formally studied. Selfishness roots, to some extent, in the uncontrollability of leisure activities. They engender in participants the desire to engage in them beyond the time or the money (if not both) available for free-time interests. That is leisure enthusiasts are often eager to spend more time at and money on the core activity than is likely to be countenanced by certain important others who also makes demands on that time and money. The latter may conclude, sooner or later, that the enthusiast is more enamored of the core leisure activity than of, say, the partner or spouse. When a participant, seemingly out of control, takes on too much of the activity, imputations of selfishness (whether overtly made or covertly held) from certain important others is surely just around the corner. This is the negative side of selfishness and its impact on positive relationships and small groups (e.g., families, friendship groups).

What, then, is the positive side? The answer, in brief, is that, as argued earlier in this chapter, serious leisure, even when selfish, is still community involvement. And such involvement helps generate social capital. But do these lofty ends – e.g., providing the community with amateur theater, volunteering for the Salvation Army, volunteering for the Olympic Games—justify the selfish means by which they are sometimes reached? Do the ends justify selfishness or other contentious practices along the way? More broadly, what is the moral basis of the positive process of community involvement?

The Moral Basis of Community Involvement

A positive sociology cannot ignore the values and related moral issues that bear on the pursuit of those things in life that people want, the things they search for that make their existence attractive and worth living. To the contrary, these must be examined, for to be "out of sync" with them holds out the possibility of diluting, if not effacing, the sense of positiveness being sought. People who engage in activities, however fulfilling, that place them at odds with society's values and morals, must occasionally face the difficult task of trying to justify their questionable pursuits. Furthermore searching for the good things in life can be powerfully motivated, with the devil taking the hindmost.

We turn first to the issue of values. Which values relate to a positive existence as achieved through the pursuit of complex leisure (i.e., serious and project-based forms)? Writing on the theory of American cultural values, Robin Williams (2000, p. 146) lists several that are clearly realizable through such free-time activity, most notably achievement, success, freedom, activity (involvement in something), and individual personality.

Although I know of no research that actually demonstrates that those who go in for complex leisure believe they have achieved something important and that they are successful, it seems reasonable to conclude that most would feel precisely this way about these two values. After all, compared with others in their reference groups, they have developed considerable knowledge and skill and acquired considerable experience, all of which they have applied with a certain level of creativity or innovation. Still many enthusiasts in this area, unlike some kinds of paid workers, cannot measure their achievement and success in remunerative terms. Rather their principal rewards include prestige, fulfillment, and the satisfaction of being altruistic.

The very nature of all leisure—that it is non-coerced activity—speaks to the level of freedom that participants find there. So nothing more need be said about this value. As for the next one—activity—complex leisure does provide for its realization in the form of a dynamic, busy pursuit grounded in one or more core activities. By contrast casual leisure, most of which is entirely or primarily inactive, cannot meet this value. True, watching television and lounging on the beach, for instance, are sometimes referred to as "activities," but they are essentially inactive activities. Better they be known as pastimes.

Finally complex leisure helps its participants realize very well the value of individual personality, quite possibly better than many kinds of employment and certainly better than casual leisure. These participants are individuated primarily by their exceptional skill, knowledge, and experience as creatively or innovatively expressed in the core activities of their pursuits. They are further individuated by their uncommon social identity as accomplished people in particular respected leisure activities (e.g., amateur golf, hobbyist stamp collecting, volunteer work with handicapped children).

The values considered so far in this section have been presented as cultural values. They are interrelated in complex ways with the values referred to in chapter 1 as the personal and social rewards of serious leisure (they are also applicable to devotee work and project-based leisure). This second group of values inspires the individual leisure participant, and in a certain sense, some of them give concrete expression to the cultural values just mentioned. For instance, the cultural value of individual personality is realized through the value-reward of self-image, while the cultural values of achievement and success gain expression, depending on the activity, through the value-rewards of self-actualization, self-expression, group accomplishment, and contribution to the group. The culture value of activity finds its individual counterpart in the value-reward of self-expression.

Moral Standards

Rather than get mired down in a discussion of the wider, often philosophical, issue of morality, I want to approach the moral facet of the pursuit of the above-mentioned values from the more down-to-earth angle of moral standards. A moral standard is a principle of human conduct that, relative to a given issue, sets out what is right and wrong, good and bad. It is the community's moral standards which help its members interpret whether community involvement motivated by the pursuit of some or all of these cultural and personal values has gone too far. Whether it has crossed the line separating good from bad. Charles Taylor puts the matter this way:

> The agent seeking significance in life, trying to define him- or herself meaningfully, has to exist in a horizon of important questions. That is what is self-defeating in modes of contemporary culture that concentrate on self-fulfillment in opposition to the demands of society, or nature, which shut out history and the bonds of solidarity. These self-centred "narcissistic" forms are indeed shallow and trivialized; they are "flattened and narrowed," as Bloom says. But this is not because they belong to the culture of authenticity. Rather it is because they fly in the face of its requirements....

Otherwise put, I can define my identity only against the background of things that matter. But to bracket out history, nature, society, the demands of solidarity, everything what I find in myself, would be to eliminate all candidates for what matters (Taylor, 1999, p. 40).

When does the quest for achievement, success, freedom, activity, and individual personality and their personal counterparts as these relate to community involvement become morally wrong?

Generally speaking the drive for achievement and success in complex leisure (and, for that matter, in devotee work), to the extent that they are reached selfishly, crosses the line of moral acceptability. More precisely this transgression undermines community involvement in the measure that it exploits people in groups, organizations, social movements, and so on and not simply one person, such as a spouse, relative, or friend. For instance, a woman who wants so strongly to be elected to the board of directors of a local charity that she tries to buy votes among the electorate of the organization is acting immorally in her community involvement. A man who believes the conductor of his community orchestra is going to name a rival as the next principal of the cello section and who spreads malicious gossip about that person in hope the conductor will grow discouraged and leave is behaving likewise. To be sure, selfishly exploiting a spouse or friend also raises a moral flag, but our focus in this chapter is on the communal impact of such behavior.

The considerable scope that leisure in democratic countries allows for freely pursuing activities raises the prospect of citizen involvement inimical to the interests of the wider community. Certain kinds of deviant leisure give credence to this possibility. Thus, anarchism – a genre of political deviance – is also a kind of serious leisure (career volunteering) leading, in this instance, to involvements in the community aimed at undermining its legitimate governmental structure. Or consider involvement in and adherence to certain kinds of deviant science (Stebbins, 1996b, pp. 231-238), which may also be conceived of as serious leisure of the amateur variety. Thus, extrasensory perception in its several forms, among them clairvoyance (knowledge gained by means other than the senses) and telepathy (mind reading), offers a nonconformist alternative to established psychology. By the way, casual leisure is not without examples of deviant communal participation scorned by some segments of the larger society (e.g., raves, defamatory postings on the Internet, organizations promoting deviance—e.g., Club Eros Swingers Club for Couples, www.cluberos.ca). Nonetheless, as noted earlier, their lack of significant voluntary altruism disqualifies them as examples of community involvement.

Turning to activity, all the values covered in this section are realized in activities and in expression of our skills, abilities, and the like through those activities. And, it may happen that people searching for valued activity, find one which, while positive to them as individuals, operates as a negative force in the larger community. Each of the preceding examples in this section centers on a core activity, thereby further exemplifying some of the ways activity as a cultural value may be seen to harm instead of help the community.

Lastly there is the value of individual personality/self-image. We value being distinctive persons, though for all but hermits, our distinctiveness must be favorably viewed by our reference group. Still, from the standpoint of community involvement, quests for distinctiveness may get out of hand, undermining collective interests instead of supporting or advancing them. Again leisure offers no small number of possibilities. For instance long-term devotion as a "pioneer" (Chabot in Hamel, 2003, p. 9) to promoting swinging in Quebec has given Jean Hamel a reputation like few others, but his kind of activity has also, in the eyes of some members of the larger community, threatened to weaken the institution of the family (Gagnon and Simon, 2005, pp. 72-73). The same may be said for Rosie O'Donnell, who as an entertainer and lesbian crusading for the cause of female homosexuality, has established herself as a special public person. Meanwhile those defending traditional family values see her, too, as a deviant and a menace (see Reiss, 1986, pp. 163-164).

Care and Community Involvement

Caring has been defined as the process of assuming personal responsibility for others' welfare, accomplished by acknowledging their needs and acting responsively toward them (Smith, Stebbins & Dover, 2006, p. 34). According to Wuthnow (1991) caring is motivated, in substantial part, by compassion, or the sympathy generated by feeling another person's suffering. Compassion leads to an inclination to show mercy for or give aid to—i.e., to care for—that person.

Assuming a person is compassionate about another's situation in life and, as a result, wants to care for that individual, what roles and associated activities are open to the first? So far I have been able to identify three. One role is occupational; some workers who are compassionate about other people make a living, at least in significant part, by caring for them, something often done as a professional calling (e.g., clergy, physicians, social workers). Viewed from the perspective of a positive sociology, many of these people would likely describe themselves as occupational devotees. Occupational caring is not community involvement, however, since the latter is the province of voluntary action.

A second role, albeit one available outside work, is caring for other people as a personal obligation. Here the caring individual, fired by compassion, feels a moral duty to care for another person or class of people. Personal caring, as I will explain more fully in the next paragraph, is predominantly disagreeable; it is therefore not leisure. Rather it is the lot of those who, though they would rather be doing something else, find themselves caring, as an example, for an ailing relative or close friend or who feel morally pressured to aid the needy at home or abroad.

These activities happen in the domain of non-work obligation, and as such, are negative rather than positive. This brings up the question of whether communal expressions of personal obligation are also instances of community involvement. My answer, which some readers may think debatable, is that these expressions are as, community involvement, marginal, primarily because the coerced nature of personal obligation signals an absence of voluntary altruism as defined earlier in this chapter. Otherwise, however, communal personal obligation seems to meet the six criteria for determining voluntary altruism.

Leisure caring is our third role. It refers to people engaged in uncoerced compassionate activity during free time, which they want to do and, in either a satisfying or a fulfilling way (or both), use their abilities and resources to succeed at doing (the general definition of leisure inherent in this statement was presented more fully in chap. 1). Both leisure caring and some kinds of personal obligation bear directly on community involvement. But leisure caring is differentiated from its occupational and personal counterparts by, among other qualities, the fact that only it is undertaken in free time. Note, however, that there may well be obligations in leisure caring, even while serious leisure research has demonstrated through several studies (Stebbins, 1992) that the obligations felt there, because they are agreeable, are defined by committed participants as minor, as "minimal." But they are real nonetheless, even if the powerful rewards of the activity significantly outweigh them and the participant has the option to quit the activity at a convenient point in the near future. In other words, serious leisure has often been found to contain some flexible obligation, or a relative freedom to honor commitments. This condition is generally missing in occupational caring and personal obligation (a somewhat deeper discussion of care as leisure is available in Stebbins, 2008a).

There can be no doubt that leisure caring, using our definition, is a type of community involvement. Motivated by compassion and altruism, caring volunteers (they may be pursuing any of the three forms of leisure) arrange for some sort of beneficial contact with the target of their care. This may be a one-shot, perhaps, spontaneous act—a good deed—such as buying a homeless person a meal or giving first-aid to a pedestrian injured in a fall.[2] Or such care may be sustained over a period of time, as in ministering to a friend dying of terminal cancer or helping out weekly at a local food bank. Consistent with our definition of volunteering presented in chapter 1, caring as volunteer activity is carried out beyond the volunteer's family. This condition means that leisure care within the family circle must be conceptualized in terms other than volunteering. Conceiving of it as special genre of family leisure—that is, as part of life there not experienced as disagreeable obligation—would be one way of achieving this.

Conclusion

If community involvement is, as claimed at the beginning of this chapter, a warm and fuzzy idea, it is simultaneously an immensely complex one. It has many positive and negative features. It includes certain kinds of social leisure—some serious, some project-based, and some casual—but excludes the purely individualist expressions of these same three. The social, though hedonic, types of casual leisure also fall beyond the purview of community involvement (the exception is casual volunteering). What is more this process is advanced in many ways on the Internet.

But, given that leisure lies at the heart of community involvement and that leisure also generates egocentric tendencies in some of its participants, selfishness presents a seemingly intractable moral problem for all concerned. Stated briefly: is selfishness in the interest of pursuing positive community involvement justifiable? What about the lot of the victim of such action? Does exploitative self-interest constitute a blot on the warm and fuzzy reputation of community involvement? Does care at the level of community involvement serve as an antidote to the sense of being selfishly exploited by an important other, in the sense that both parties, in this scenario, are now altruistically participating directly and indirectly in reaching the noble goal of communal compassionate care?

The tension between selfishness and community involvement may never be possible to wholly resolve for most people in most situations. Yet it may be possible to reduce significantly its effect such as by gaining a sufficient grasp of what counts most in life. Where do our interests really lie? Is it possible that, in striving for the positive things in life, as set out in the preceding chapters, we might also achieve the sort of outlook on that life that at least dampens or channels personal tendencies toward selfishness? This is the main theme of the final chapter.

Notes

1. See also "The amateur's hour, or why the tool-bench inventors, self-schooled savants, Internet nighthawks and all the rest of the utterly eccentric non-pros are the last, best embodiment of American independence." New York Times Magazine, 1 July.
2. Good Samaritan acts of bystander intervention exemplify further this type of care (Darley & Latané, 1967).

7

What Really Counts?

*"It has been said that the love of money is the root of all evil.
The want of money is so quite as truly"—Samuel Butler, Erewhon
(1872)*

Most adults must live by their work, even while they live for their leisure. Moreover, for some of them, there is precious little leisure to live for, a problem we highlighted in chapter 3 when addressing ourselves to the balance of work, leisure, and obligation. That is it is a problem for all workers save the occupational devotee, for whom work is essentially leisure.

There are forces that drive people to work, despite their craving for leisure and the fact that they lose time for the second in prioritizing the "necessity" of the first. In this chapter we look further at these forces and this question of necessity. Here, I put materialism in its place as a necessary evil for most people, even today. Meanwhile personal fulfillment and well-being are among the more profound and lasting goals people may also have. These latter two are strongly positive features of life. With such goals in mind what counts is finding either an optimal leisure lifestyle (OLL) or an optimal positive lifestyle (OPL), if not both. The two maximize the attractive side of everyday life, while minimizing unwanted tension with important others (e.g., employer, family, friends). What counts is finding work (which may require leaving one or more jobs in search of it) that is not so disagreeable that the worker rues Mondays, celebrates Fridays, finds holidays too short, but hangs on because of the money. To be sure, money buys an existence, but its relationship to happiness is far more complicated. The individual of tomorrow, said as we view the future of work, leisure, and obligation, will be essentially *homo otiosus* – leisure man—not *homo faber* (the concept of *homo otiosus* includes, but is significantly broader than, *homo ludens* [Huizinga, 1955] and *homo voluntas* [Smith, 2000]).

In the present chapter I examine a set of human personal and social problems that spring up when the conditions on which positive life depends are lacking or undermined. Absence of these conditions spawns, for example, alienation, boredom, burnout, personal stress, friction in positive relationships and the personal and collective consequences of these. My object here is to present some strategies for solving these problems, through promoting arrangements and conditions that foster, as much as possible, positive personal attitudes in the activities that make up our lifestyles in the three domains.

How Necessary is Work?

Unlike occupational devotees who are paid so they may work, it is the opposite for most people: they work so they may be paid. When work is uninteresting, but still decently remunerative, workers can at least sustain life and, with any leftover money, enjoy a bit the smorgasbord of consumer opportunities the commercial world lays out before them. A lifetime of uninteresting work is a high price to pay for economic survival and some spending cash, but many a modern worker enters into precisely this bargain with his educational qualifications and personal standards for occupational success.

Still, the relationship of remuneration to the three domains of life is complicated, as is evident in the different economic situations that workers both live in and hope to live in. The following disquisition on economic situation is an extension to all workers of the concept as initially applied only to occupational devotees (see Stebbins, 2004a, pp. 91-100). Nonetheless, as a key embodiment of positive sociology in action in the domain of work, the devotees must remain part of the discussion.

Economic Situation

Economic situation" is my term for the level of living made possible by a person's disposable wealth, that being for most people occupational income, but for a minority of them, it includes returns on investments. Applied to work, economic situation can be conceptualized as arrayed along a scale of increasing wealth that runs from poverty to opulence. The low end of the scale is anchored in *poverty* and *near poverty*, where the worker is desperately trying to make a living, but so far with little monetary success. Here is the home of the starving artist and the minimally successful small business proprietor. Indeed for occupational devotees money earned at their work is problematic only, though still very profoundly, in that there is little or none of it. Life for them is sustained by supplementary work, much of it more or less unskilled such as driving a taxi or delivering pizzas.

With some financial success struggling workers are wafted up the economic situation scale toward the level of *passable living*. Here they are joined by other kinds of workers, most of whom are just starting out in their chosen line of work and who have had the good fortune to avoid the poverty stage. In the world of occupational devotion, moderately successful artists and others share the passable living level with newly minted apprentice tradesmen, consultants and counselors fresh from university programs who have just hung out their shingles, and the owners of recently inaugurated small businesses who, from the beginning, have managed to turn a decent profit. Passable living consists, in the main, of having reasonably nutritious meals on a regular basis, lodging in a passably safe and healthy social and physical environment, and enough free time beyond work hours for adequate bodily maintenance (e.g., sleep, exercise) as well as relaxation and personal development through leisure.

With still greater monetary success, workers enjoying a passable living may advance farther up the economic situation scale to the realm of *comfortable living*. Living comfortably builds on the base of passable living, by adding significant discretionary income with which to buy a variety of consumer goods that make life easier and more enjoyable than was possible during passable existence. This includes expanding one's personal definition of the good life to include acquisitions that go well beyond minimum standards, such as a house though an apartment would do, a Cadillac when a Ford would do, or designer clothes when mass produced apparel would do. Although many occupational devotees, in the course of their careers, eventually reach this level of economic existence, some actually start out more or less on it. Graduates from training programs in the most lucrative professions, among them law, medicine, engineering, and computer science, offer some fine examples. That is, unless they are saddled with huge educational debts the retirement of which might force them into passable living for some years. And it is not impossible that, once in awhile, a devotee small business is a roaring success from the outset, as could happen with an instantly profitable restaurant or family farm (following a few good, back-to-back growing years).

Perched at the top end of the economic situation scale is *opulent living*. Workers at these lofty heights enjoy amounts of discretionary cash far in excess of their counterparts at the next lowest level. Opulence permits conspicuous consumption. It also permits investments of various sorts, which in good economic times enable these workers to acquire other sources of wealth in addition to the revenue they receive directly from pursuing the core activity of their occupation. This situation, we shall see shortly, also gives occupational devotees a certain flexibility, or margin of maneuver, when it comes to sticking to purely devotee activities or seeking extra income by working part of the time at less fulfilling, albeit decently, paying employment. Whereas very few occupational devotees start out at this level, some do advance this far up the economic situation scale. Most who do are in the sports and entertainment fields or, more rarely, one of the lucrative professions.

This economic situation scale is an objective tool, intended to foster understanding of the way workers, in general, and occupational devotees, in particular, are distributed along the dimension of wealth. To give the scale greater precision, future empirical work in this area should include some quantitative measures of its four levels. Meanwhile, subjectively speaking, individual workers may define themselves differently, which seems especially likely among those living passably or comfortably near the middle of the scale. For example, some might be inclined to argue that, even if science objectively classifies them as enjoying a comfortable living, they feel they are really only just getting by on the passable level.

Occupational Devotion, Serious Leisure, and Money

There are three critical orientations toward the question of pay for devotee work, a complexity in this area that is unknown in the other spheres of work. One I will dub the *principled orientation*: occupational devotees and would-be devotees seek pay for pursuing their core activity, so they can do it more often than they can as serious leisure enthusiasts. They seek to be paid so they may work. The second orientation—label it the *acquisitive orientation*—is that devotees and would-be devotees see their occupation as offering a comfortable living, perhaps even an opulent one; that is, it is a job offering substantially greater remuneration than needed to live passably. They work so they may be paid; they see their remuneration as high enough to allow for an elevated standard living. The personal plan directing these devotees is to eventually abandon their fulfilling work for work returning substantial extrinsic rewards, thereby giving substance to Sophocles' observation: "there's nothing in the world so demoralizing as money." The third orientation combines the first two—it is the *principled-acquisitive orientation*; motivated by this disposition devotees seek to be paid so they may work, but at the same time, see no reason why they cannot sooner or later achieve at least a comfortable living in the bargain.

This is the field on which occupational devotion is put to test. At which point, if ever, does the devotee sell his occupational soul to the monetary devil? When does making more money take precedence over performing, more or less exclusively, fulfilling work? This is a personal decision, which it is hoped the following pages can help inform.

Before we leave this discussion of work and money, it is in order to ask about people who just love to make money, for the reason, joined with others, of showing how well they can master the challenge of doing so. This challenge is possibly most commonly found in running a profitable enterprise or successfully playing the stock market. To the extent that this activity is part of a person's job, both may be classified as occupational devotion. Still some people take up such a challenge in their free time, as a hobby (activity participation type). After a day's work, and for some in retirement, these "monetary hobbyists" settle in for session after session of such core activities as reviewing market trends, buying and selling shares, and reading up on new investment possibilities. They treat the amount of money they make as evidence of their knowledge and experience in this field, akin to an amateur's athlete's trophies or the long-service awards of a career volunteer.[1]

Money and Happiness

If both the presence of money and its lack lead to evil, as Samuel Butler affirmed in this chapter's epigraph, might it be that the stuff really does buy happiness, or in the preferred language of this volume, might it buy well-being which, in turn, leads to a positive existence? Many a popular book and magazine article trumpets an affirmative answer to this question, and then serves up advice on how this may be accomplished.[2] But these are, in effect, only manuals; they are not studies backed by data showing that, whatever the means, money sometimes, or always, buys happiness. On the one hand, then, the manuals fail to offer convincing evidence that the formulae listed within lead to the promised land of wealth-based joy.

On the other hand, there *is* evidence demonstrating that certain non-material factors bear on the human happiness quotient, and that money may, under some conditions, actually hinder our pursuit of happiness. For example, Oswald and Powdthavee (2007) found that half the British population view themselves as overweight, and that happiness and mental health are worse among fatter people in Britain and Germany than among thinner folk. A partial explanation for this situation, say the authors, is that economic prosperity weakens self-control, encouraging some people to eat too much, which then undermines subjective well-being. Taking a different tack Layard (2005, chap. 4) singles out our tendency toward social comparison with oneself and others as the basis for the unhappiness of many people with their own, comparable position of wealth. He concludes that "one 'secret to happiness' is to enjoy things as they are, without comparing them with anything better." In other words, happiness is not found in trying to keep up with the Joneses. Another secret is to discover which things really make us happy (Layard, 2005, p. 53), what really counts.

Layard (2005, p. 12) defines happiness as "feeling good – enjoying life and wanting the feeling to be maintained." Elsewhere in this book happiness has been considered under the headings of subjective and social well-being, two staples of the serious leisure perspective. Unhappiness (lack of well-being), Layard says, is opposite of this, feeling bad and wishing things were different. Seligman (2003) brings us to the jumping off point for a positive sociology and the role of happiness therein when he argues that "authentic happiness" comes from realizing our potential for enduring self-fulfillment. And, from what I have been saying about fulfillment in this book, it should be easy to conclude that, much of the time, no direct link exists between it and money. The sociology of consumption further explains this observation.

Distinguishing Consumption and Leisure

Let us start by noting that a substantial amount of consumption today has little or nothing to do with leisure and its basis for fulfillment. Examples are legion: buying toothpaste, life insurance, accounting services, natural gas for home heating, transit tickets for getting to work, and on and on. Such consumption, call it *obligatory consumption*, however practically important for consumers, lies beyond the scope of this discussion. As for the other areas of consumption, the relationship of this process with leisure is often complicated.

In these other areas – in *leisure-based consumption*—a critical distinction to make is whether the leisure component of a particular activity is directly and solely dependent on the acquisition of a thing or service (e.g., buying a CD, concert ticket, or a session of massage) or whether purchase of something is but a prerequisite to a set of conditions that, much more centrally, shapes the activity as a leisure experience. In other words, is consumption an initiator of a leisure experience or a facilitator of such experience? In *initiatory, leisure-based consumption* a person buys, for instance, a ticket enabling entrance to a cinema, a CD enabling listening to recorded music, a new sporty car enabling pleasurable motoring, or a club membership enabling fine drinking and dining with valued members. In such consumption, the purchaser proceeds more or less directly to use of the purchased item. Here leisure and consumption do seem to be inextricably linked – an identity – even while sense of the initial consumption may fade as the owner replays for the tenth time the CD or drives six months later the flashy new automobile.

Not so with *facilitative, leisure-based consumption*. Here the acquired item only sets in motion a set of activities, which when completed, enable the purchaser to use the item in a satisfying or fulfilling leisure experience. As an example note that amateur violinists, if they are to play at all, must first rent or purchase a violin—an act of acquisition. Yet their most profound leisure experience is competently and artistically playing music and, earlier, practicing to accomplish this, all of which costs nothing, though, obviously, it is, clearly, only possible to do with the acquired instrument (a consumer product). Moreover this profound leisure experience might be further facilitated by buying music lessons and paying for public transit tickets to get to the teacher's studio.

In this last example, one or more consumer purchases or rentals are necessary steps to experiencing the leisure being sought. Still leisure activities exist for which no facilitative consumption whatsoever is needed for participation in them. There are areas in free time where consumption and leisure are clearly separate spheres. It is in the free-time sphere that we find *non-consumptive leisure*. As an example consider the variety of hobbies, among them, the liberal arts reading hobbies (e.g., reading a kind of history or science), some collecting hobbies (e.g., leaves, seashells, insects), and some outdoor sport and activities (e.g., playing soccer or touch football, walking in nature, swimming in a lake). (For further discussion of the concepts in leisure studies that show in detail the complex relationship of leisure and consumption, see Stebbins, 2008b)

Finding satisfaction and fulfillment using money as a means to this end nevertheless hinges on living in an economic situation that makes this possible. Those in poverty and near poverty and some in passable living lack this resource. In their situation an absence of money is a root of at least some evil, perhaps in their eyes, all evil. Keeping up with the Joneses and the unhappiness that accompanies this process is not their problem, which can only begin farther up the scale with comfortable living.

Finding Balance in Life

This goal was addressed in chapter 3. There I set out several strategies for finding ways to maximize the positive side of life while minimizing its negative sides. Eschewing the monetary treadmill that leads to unhappiness, as previously described, is accomplished, in part, by living according to the pertinent standards propagated by the strategy of voluntary simplicity. What we must consider now is the moral issue of selfishness: finding this balance is illusory if, in searching for it, important others feel exploited and then succeed in negotiating with the participant the charge of being selfish.

From the statement in chapter 1 about costs and rewards, it is evident why the desire to participate in the core amateur, hobbyist, or volunteer activity can become for some participants some of the time quite *uncontrollable*. This happens because it engenders in those people a desire to engage in the activity beyond the time or the money (if not both) available for it. As a professional violinist once counseled his daughter, "Rachel, never marry an amateur violinist! He will want to play quartets all night" (from Bowen, 1935, p. 93). There seems to be an almost universal desire to upgrade: to own a better set of golf clubs, buy a more powerful telescope, take more dance lessons perhaps from a renowned (and consequently more expensive) professional, and so forth. The same applies to some hobbyist and volunteer pursuits.

Chances are good, therefore, that some serious leisure enthusiasts will be eager to spend more time at and money on the core activity than is likely to be countenanced by certain important others who also makes demands on that time and money. The latter may soon arrive at the interpretation that the enthusiast is more enamored of the core leisure activity than of, say, the partner or spouse.[3] It follows that accusations of selfishness may not be long off. I found in my research on serious leisure that highly attractive activity and selfishness are natural partners (Stebbins, 2001a, chap. 4). Whereas some casual leisure and even project-based leisure can also be uncontrollable, the marginality hypothesis (stated below) implies that such a proclivity is generally significantly stronger among serious leisure participants. Unfortunately for research in the area, selfishness is an ethical question seldom raised in leisure studies.

Furthermore, I have argued over the years that amateurs, and sometimes even the activities they pursue, are *marginal* in society, for amateurs are neither dabblers (casual leisure) nor professionals (see also Stebbins, 1979). Moreover, studies of hobbyists and career volunteers show that they and some of their activities are just as marginal and for many of the same reasons (Stebbins, 1996a; 1998b). Several properties of serious leisure give substance to these observations. One, although seemingly illogical according to common sense, is that serious leisure is characterized empirically by an important degree of positive commitment to a pursuit (Stebbins, 1992, pp. 51-52). This commitment is measured, among other ways, by the sizeable investments of time and energy in the leisure made by its devotees and participants. Two, serious leisure is pursued with noticeable intentness, with such passion that Erving Goffman (1963, pp. 144-145) once categorized amateurs and hobbyists as the "quietly disaffiliated." People with such orientations toward their leisure are marginal compared with people who go in for the ever-popular forms of much of casual leisure. Both types are capable of generating selfish behavior.

All the foregoing also applies to devotee work, although the necessity of making a living may, in some instances, blunt interpretations of selfishness hurled by potential victims as they mull the ethical implications of the self-seeker's actions. Nevertheless, this "necessity of making a living" or of moving up the economic situation scale from basic needs into the vortex of keeping up with the Joneses can also be conceived of as selfish behavior when the exploited person fails to accept this goal. Thus, a wife might complain that her husband's desire to work more (as devotee or not) primarily benefits him and much less his family, whom his wife sees as deteriorating because of his habitual absence most days and nights of the week.

As pointed out earlier, herein lies a perturbing ethical problem. Being victim of selfishness is disagreeable and being labeled as selfish is likewise unpleasant. For people suffering from the second, the positiveness gained from pursuing leisure or devotee work is noticeably diluted. True, for some selfish workers and participants in leisure, this charge is, as it were, water off a duck's back. Either they flatly reject that charge or they have little concern for what the victim thinks of their behavior. Others might treat the charge as a cost of their occupational or free-time pursuit, but not one sufficiently powerful to persuade them to change their ways. But still others might well see the victim's point, and, valuing the positive relationship between the two, try to reduce, if not fully eliminate, the grounds for it. It is in the last scenario that the (formerly) selfish person gains the greatest measure of positiveness.

When Positiveness Fails to Take Root

Since the beginning of this book, I have been exploring in diverse ways how the attitude of positiveness may be experienced in everyday life. First we examined its place in the balance of work, leisure, and obligation. Then we considered its role in personal development, self confidence, and communal development. But what happens when these various favorable conditions are wholly absent or absent to such an extent that positiveness fails to take root for an individual? What happens when negativeness is the dominant outlook on life?

On the most general plane, a negative outlook on life, or at minimum an outlook containing very little positiveness, is one of some combination of desperation, restlessness, perhaps anger, hate, or fear, in any case a package of negative emotions and personal states. Or, seen through the lens of the preceding section, people who think negatively about their existence are unhappy.

More particularly, both negativeness and positiveness must be seen as held in degrees. In other words, life, for most people, is more or less negative or positive; they are more or less happy or unhappy. Close examination of a given individual would seldom find this person to be purely positive or negative. And, it should be clear that, whatever the degree with which these two attitudes are held, they are subjective views of life, even if occasionally supported by selected objective indicators. Thus, one man's negativeness, say, because he sees his car as too plebeian, is another's positiveness, because for him, having a car of any kind (that runs) is a luxury.

To the extent that we may treat happiness as an expression of positiveness (the first is an emotion, the second an attitude), a couple of international surveys chart the global distribution of the former (*Economist*, 2007a). One of them asked a standard question: "how satisfied are you with your life, on a scale of nought to ten" (p. 63). With certain exceptions people in rich parts of the world (e.g., Japan, Europe, North America) responded much more often by describing themselves as satisfied than those in poor parts (e.g., most African states), suggesting in a general way that wealth and happiness are positively correlated. A similar pattern was also evident between rich and poor citizens within countries. All this, by the way, does not invalidate the observation made earlier that finding satisfaction and fulfillment using money as a means to this end nevertheless hinges on living in an economic situation that facilitates this process (see also Layard, 2005, chap. 5). The rich, compared with the poor, seem still to be relatively happy, even while some of them suffer occasional unhappiness when they fail to match, if not out do, the Joneses.

Conditions of Negativeness

This subsection could be filled with material sufficient for another book, so fecund is contemporary Western civilization of conditions for personal negativeness. Thus a sample of these conditions will have to do; below I will treat of: boredom, burnout, alienation, personal stress, and friction in positive relationships. Discussion of them should give adequate weight to the proposition that, when sufficient positiveness fails to take root, negativeness, like a robust weed, thrives nicely in the garden of life. Bear in mind, as we go along, that negativeness is a cardinal antecedent of many of the problems around which problem-centered sociology revolves. This will be the subject of the next and final section of the present chapter.

Boredom is an emotional state of mind rooted, for the bored individual, in an acute absence of meaning of objects, activities, and life's everyday situations, as understood within his system of values and the larger culture (Stebbins, 2003). Looking at it from a somewhat different angle, Brissett and Snow (1993) argue that boredom is born of either lack of momentum or lack of psychological engagement with the events at hand. In any case, meaninglessness and absence of momentum experienced as boredom are, for many so afflicted, strong motivators to find meaning, even if, in some instances, the meaning found brings risk, deviance, conflict, and the like—in a word, more negativeness.

Obviously, boredom does not spring exclusively from inactivity ("nothing to do"); it may also arise from activity, which alas, is uninteresting, unstimulating. Moreover, as might be expected, such activity is necessarily obligatory, whether carried out at work or in the domain of non-work obligation; it is a feature most unskilled jobs as well as certain domestic tasks (common examples include washing dishes and preparing routine meals). Boredom, then, is hardly a feature of life unique to the domain of free time.

Burnout, in a way, stands opposite to boredom, in the sense that it is a kind of overstimulation rather than under-stimulation. It has been defined as physical and emotional exhaustion stemming from long-term stress, frustration, and excessive obligation in a volunteer role (Smith, Stebbins & Dover, 2006, p. 30). In fact burnout is not confined to volunteers, but may occur in work or other leisure (serious or project-based). When boredom strikes complex leisure, the second undergoes a metamorphosis, turning into overbearing obligation and taking on a work-like quality too unpleasant to bear in an activity once pursued for its significant level of fulfillment. Burnout has much the same effect in the devotee occupations, and is disliked for many of the same reasons. By contrast, when it occurs in non-devotee work, it is more purely a matter of exhaustion, too many hours put in on the job or working at it too intensely, with too few hours available to recover from accumulating fatigue (see "overworking" in Kalleberg, 2007, chap. 6). The earlier example of overworked physicians, even though they are devotees, still nicely illustrates this point.

Many years ago, Seeman (1972) isolated six types of *alienation*, which serve well our goal of identifying some of the conditions of negativeness present in modern society. The six types are

1. alienation as *powerlessness,* or the sense of little control versus the mastery of events;
2. alienation as *meaninglessness*, or the sense of incomprehensibility versus understanding the events of one's life;
3. alienation as *normlessness*, or high commitment to unconventional means versus high commitment to conventional means of achieving goals;
4. *cultural estrangement*; or individual rejection of commonly held values in the society versus commitment to existing group standards;
5. *self-estrangement*, or individual engagement in activities that are intrinsically unrewarding versus intrinsic involvement in a task or activity; and
6. *social isolation*, or the sense of exclusion or rejection versus acceptance.

By and large, these six are self-explanatory. Still it should be understood that 3 and 4 refer primarily to deviant behavior, leisure or not. Number 5 expresses a standard Marxian conception of alienation, which by the way, cannot logically issue from devotee work or from any genre of leisure.

Personal stress, as examined here, results from trying to cope with one or more of life's problems. More specifically it is a physical or mental condition, if not both, that develops when an individual makes a substantial and enduring attempt to remedy a particular, unavoidable disturbance in everyday existence. Some of the conditions of negativeness considered in this section are too diffuse to be seen as sources of stress. Others, however, are clearly antecedents of it, including burnout, friction in positive relationships, and depending on circumstances, any of the six types of alienation.

The stress we are discussing is unwanted, or bad, tension, and it should not be confused with what we might call "good" tension. The latter is common in, for example, sport and the performing arts, where it sometimes takes the form of nerves or stage fright. Furthermore the flow experience in work and leisure sometimes contains an element of tension, particularly in the fifth of the eight components of flow: sense of deep, focused involvement in the activity (see chap. 1). Here there is a tension to stay focused, to concentrate, so as to avoid playing a wrong note in music, forgetting a line in theater, missing a crucial maneuver in kayaking, failing to see the unfolding of a play in football, and so on. Tension in these activities comes from trying to keep all outside thoughts from redirecting elsewhere the all-important single-mindedness of the moment.

Friction in positive relationships is our final example of the conditions of personal negativeness. It refers to personal stress arising from some sort of discord with an important other, a spouse, relative, close friend, colleague at work, among others. What is particularly upsetting about such friction is that it temporarily destroys a special zone of positiveness in the lives of those affected by it. Selfishness is the cause of some of this tension, as when acrimonious argument erupts over a wife spending too much time away from her husband in nights out with the "girls." Or when the weekend male couch potato, glued as he is to the usual string of sportscasts on television at that time, is happily savoring his domestic existence until his wife, tired of his continuous reluctance to rake the leaves sarcastically reminds him of his household duties.

These illustrations are relatively small instances of relational friction compared with the enduring interpersonal problems of much greater gravity that may emerge. They include ongoing spats over putative marital infidelity; expensive consumer habits; and "excessive" time committed to a hobby, amateur activity (e.g., the golf widow), or devotee work. In them it is often possible to find selfishness lurking in the background. In other instances of enduring tension in positive relationships, the source of the problem lies outside the couple, sometimes rendering the problem difficult to manage. Thus, friction may arise in a marital relationship when the employer of one of them starts demanding many more hours of work, perhaps at the same pay, or when one of them is forced into the role of caregiver for a seriously ill parent. In all these examples of serious problems, the question may eventually emerge as to whether the relationship under this sort of siege is any longer a positive one.

Consequences of Negativeness

A positive sociology must be concerned with two major types of consequence of negativeness in a society. One is individual: one or more conditions of negativeness can become a personal problem. The other is social: one or more conditions of negativeness can coalesce into a social problem.

First, however, let it be clear that I am not claiming that negativeness of the sort illustrated in the preceding section always has far-reaching consequences such that they inevitably become an enduring problem, personal or social. For it happens that some chronically bored people do manage to adapt to their situation, and some eventually find an interesting activity or two. Burnout, although most unpleasant at the time, nonetheless appears to get remedied, accomplished perhaps by quitting the overly demanding volunteer or occupational post, perhaps by successfully negotiating a more workable list of responsibilities. Relational friction may get resolved, not infrequently aided by a counsellor, or the most aggrieved party (or parties) may learn to live with the condition, possibly even taking pride in being resilient in adversity.

But, for individuals forced to suffer through long periods of negativeness, it, for all but the most stoic, is sure to eat at their sense of well-being. The more intense the unpleasant condition, the more inclined most of these people will be to try to reduce its intensity, if not completely eliminate it. So as to avoid scooping the next section, let me simply observe at this point that the behavioral consequences of enduring negativeness may, in principle, be themselves positive or negative, conformist or deviant, self-enhancing or self-defeating, and the like.

Among the dozens of personal problems consider the following sample: marital stress, occupational burnout, sex-based discrimination in the workplace, bullying at school, acrimonious parental relations with adolescent offspring, landlord-tenant grievances, and persisting disagreements with neighbors. Most of these are recognized scientifically, in that they have been studied through research and that practitioners have made available some helpful information on how to handle them. Still several non-rental landlord-tenant grievances and all neighbor-related disagreements have, to my knowledge, received little or no scholarly attention, leaving those concerned to handle on their own the tension they experience there.

When the consequences of personal problems assume a collective form, when they become social problems, the community has, by this time, come to define, or "construct," them (Spector & Kitsuse, 1987) as threatening and consequently in need of remedial action. This commonly leads it to mobilize in an attempt to reduce or eliminate them. By this point, the problem has grown from one of personal negativeness to one of personal *and* group negativeness, which as stated at the beginning of this book, has been, for years, standard grist for the sociological mill—the social problem. And, to repeat, problem-centered sociology is not exclusively focused on social problems, since it is also delves into the personal problems mentioned above as well as the problems in contemporary life that fit poorly the conventional conception of social problem (e.g., terrorism, revolution, failings of the democratic state). As for social problems, as conventionally conceived of, they include those having to do with health (e.g., care, disease), mental disorder, sexuality (e.g., pornography, prostitution), alcohol and drug use, and crime. Also part of this list are violence, poverty and homelessness, racial and ethnic discrimination, education (e.g., low quality, underfunding), urban living (e.g., pollution, traffic congestion), population (e.g., overpopulation, underpopulation), environmental issues, and war.

Negativeness and Positive Sociology

What can a positive sociology do for people facing personal or social problems beyond what problem-centered sociology is already trying to do? Beyond studying and attempting to ameliorate those problems? Before tackling these questions I wish to repeat that a positive sociology is not inherently problem-centered, as the idea of problem has been considered in this book. Positive sociology is the study of what people want, of the rewarding, satisfying, fulfilling things they search for to make their existence attractive, worth living. Still positive sociology can also contribute to amelioration of a number of problems that people face today, be they personal, social, or extra-social (i.e., terrorism, revolution). To this end I will now reconsider the earlier sample of these problems, which are all personal, to show how positiveness in the lives of the people faced with them can, in various ways, be ameliorative.

Personal Problems

Let us start with the problem of boredom, whose relationship to positiveness is arguably the most obvious among all the problems in this sample. Though, as stated previously, boredom is hardly a feature of life unique to the domain of leisure, it has not gone unnoticed in leisure studies, youth studies, or research on mental health problems, particularly those of adolescents (for a review of this literature see Patterson, Pegg & Dobson-Patterson, 2000, pp. 54-59). Nor should it be ignored, given Schopenhauer's observation that "the most general survey shows us that the two foes of human happiness are pain and boredom." The research examined by Patterson and colleagues stresses the importance of leisure as a way to reduce boredom, even though there are limitations to this approach. For instance Tess Kay (1990, p. 415) cautions that boredom, lethargy, and depression are commonly the lot of the unemployed, whatever their age, and while in this situation, they typically feel that they have no right to leisure.

Other limitations appear when examining adolescent boredom. Iso-Ahola and Crowley (1991) found that wayward youth have little or no interest in repetitious and constant leisure experiences, which is characteristic of some serious leisure. But they adore casual leisure, some types of which can, for them, eliminate some of the negativeness of boredom. This relief is temporary, however, for such hedonic leisure is, by definition, fleeting. As for the serious leisure activities, all do require a significant level of perseverance, but by no means all require repetitious preparation of the kind needed to learn a musical instrument or train for a sport (Stebbins, in press). For example, none of the volunteer activities and liberal arts hobbies has repetitive features. The same may be said for amateur science, hobbyist collecting, various games, and the numerous pastimes referred to earlier as activity participation. Spelunking, orienteering, and some kinds of sports volunteering exemplify nonrepetitive serious leisure that is both exciting and, with the first two, adventurous.

This is a difficult area, as Hartmann and Massoglia (2007) observe. It exudes commonsense appeal, but the proposition that athletic activity is a deterrent to crime and delinquency lacks empirical support. One weakness of research in this field is that it has centered almost entirely on popular team sport, neglecting many of the other kinds of sport and leisure open to youth and young adults. The potential of these kinds of leisure as alternatives to crime and delinquency remains to be systematically explored.

Moving next to burnout positiveness, it turns out, is not always a feasible way to combat it. For example, two common approaches to dealing with burnout in non-devotee work, are to leave the offending employment or to stay and negotiate a less stressful routine for it. Neither is inherently positive, as this concept has been explored in this book. In fact, both are essentially problem-centered approaches. By contrast burnout in volunteering can be alleviated rather more in the spirit of positive sociology, namely, by leaving the stressful volunteer position or responsibility and taking up another that meets the volitional definition of volunteering set out in chapter 1. Whether the new role sought is casual or career volunteering depends on what the volunteer wants from this type of leisure and what personal skills, knowledge, and experience this person can bring to it (project-based leisure, short-term as it typically is, seems largely immune to burnout). And, in the event an employee has lost control over the pace of core activities constituting a devotee work role, negotiating a less stressful routine there could have a positive outcome. Regaining that control would then restore the attractive, devotee feature of the job.

Alienation by way of self-estrangement offers some fine opportunities to showcase the effectiveness of a positive approach to dealing with this personal problem. Although by no means all leisure is founded on intrinsically rewarding activity (e.g., pure chance winning in recreational gambling, watching spectator sport as a fan/consumer), most certainly the serious and project-based forms are. More precisely many of the activities falling within these two are carried out because they generate significant fulfillment for the participant, because they enable that person to experience many of the ten rewards as well as immersion in the related social world. It is also true that amateurs and hobbyists who make artistic or craft-like objects and sell them, even if sales are too meager for a livelihood, might experience a certain sense of Marxian alienation, a sense of estrangement from their products. So here, possibly, serious leisure might not offer a positive, intrinsically rewarding solution to this problem. Otherwise, however, it, project-based leisure and, I should like to add, devotee work generally provide an attractive escape from self-estrangement, which is largely, if not entirely, felt in the sort of paid employment in which workers produce things from which estrangement is possible.

Csikszentmihalyi (1990, chap. 9) offers several illustrations of how people may cope with personal stress through participation in flow-based activities. He observes:

> The peak in the development of coping skills is reached when a young man or woman has achieved a strong enough sense of self, based on personally selected goals that no external disappointment can entirely undermine who he or she is. For some people the strength derives from a goal that involves identification with the family, with the country, or with a religion or an ideology. For others, it depends on mastery of a harmonious system of symbols, such as art, music, or physics….

Why are some people weakened by stress, while others gain strength from it? Basically the answer is simple: those who know how to transform a hopeless situation into a new flow activity that can be controlled will be able to enjoy themselves, and emerge stronger from the ordeal. (p. 203)

The domain of leisure is larger than that of flow. As I have explained elsewhere (Stebbins, 2006a, p. 17), it is not uniformly present even in general activities whose core activities produce flow, and it is altogether absent in some kinds of serious leisure and much of project-based leisure. Nonetheless, both of these can help people cope with stress, much as flow helps as described above.

Positive sociology offers a solution to frictional problems in positive relationships through the mechanism of shared leisure activity. At bottom, it is about the adage: the family (friendship, etc.) that plays together stays together. Any of the three forms would seem, in general, to be effective here, in that partners in a relationship should, in principle, be capable of finding something to do in their free time that includes each other and that generates a special bond between them. Any number of possibilities exist when shared, among them, routinely viewing a spectator sport, playing musical instruments, watching films, walking in nature, working on a collection (of stamps, coins, books, etc.), preparing genealogies, taking a tour, and pursuing an amateur science. In Orthner's (1975) terminology such activities work best, in this regard, if they are "joint" rather than "parallel," since the first requires intra-couple interaction and the second does not. Going together to a spectator sporting event or a film is parallel leisure, though the couple might convert it to joint leisure by discussing after the game or the picture what they just saw.

Social Problems

Health is a social problem that positiveness can sometimes help remedy. Thus, to the extent agreeable exercise is required for effective prevention of disease or debilitating bodily and mental states, leisure and devotee work can be effective prescriptions.[4] Since the relationship between leisure and devotee work, on the one hand, and preventive medicine, on the other, was examined in chapter 5, no more need be said here about that subject. What remains to be considered in this section about health as a social problem, is identifying and implementing beneficial rehabilitation following treatment of certain medical conditions.

While leisure's contribution here is potentially enormous, determining which leisure to recommend can be difficult. In this regard I posed the following question in an article on leisure and neuro-rehabilitation

(Stebbins, in press): how can both therapists and people with neuro-disabilities find their way around in the serious leisure perspective? The point of departure I suggested was, given the disability in question, to determine which types of serious leisure and activities within those types are feasible. Next, for these feasible, serious leisure areas of the Perspective, determine which types and activities match the client's tastes, natural talents, and personal interests. That is, try to develop a list of, say, a half-dozen, serious leisure activities that offer as strong an opportunity as possible for this person to find self-fulfillment. Finally, choose one of these, or more if the person has time and energy for learning how to do them. But remember that, although the serious leisure perspective encourages participation in serious leisure activities, it certainly not do so to the exclusion of one or both of the other two forms. Thus the ultimate goal is to help clients develop an OLL or, if their work is of the devotee variety, an OPL.

Recreational abuse of alcohol and drugs are long-standing social problems in most Western countries. As leisure both types might appear, on first glance, to be positive activities. But, to the extent these substances are used in excess, used to the point where a user loses control over consumption of them, the activity becomes coerced. It is therefore, by our definition, no longer leisure; it is, instead, negative activity, with this quality often exacerbated by the fact that it also widely regarded as deviant. What, for many people, starts positively as leisure—e.g., having a few drinks, experimenting with marijuana or cocaine—for some of them finishes negatively as chemical dependence. Now the challenge is to try to restore positiveness to their lives.

That challenge is not only to solve the negative problem of dependency on the drug but also to replace it with the positive activity of leisure or devotee work, which is equal to or greater in attractiveness than that found in the first. In principle, rehabilitating reformed users by applying approximately the same approach as in neuro-rehabilitation should work. Further, serious leisure should be the most effective of the three forms at achieving this goal, in that it is the most likely to endure over a substantial period of the life course, offer the deepest self-fulfillment, bring the richest return of personal and social rewards, and therefore, generate the strongest commitment to avoid ruining these acquisitions and benefits by relapsing into uncontrollable consumption of drugs or alcohol. Finding devotee work is another positive rehabilitative solution, albeit one, when compared with leisure, that is less accessible, less realistically obtainable, for most clients.

I know of no cases where this formula has been applied, though not-withstanding the reigning American approach of punishment and custo-dial treatment for drug and alcohol abuse, I should think someone would have discovered it and tried it out. The matter is complicated, however, by the fact that cases abound of people who seem to enjoy a lifestyle akin to an OLL or OPL, but who nevertheless destroy themselves and their work or leisure careers through excessive use of such substances. The history of jazz is legendary for this sort of thing, as the lives of Chet Baker, Charlie Parker, and Billie Holiday attest. In sport (and I am not talking about use of performance-enhancing drugs) consider the drug-shattered lives of Poli Díaz (boxer—heroin), Julio Alberto (soccer player—cocaine), and Diego Armando Maradona (soccer player—heroin). Greg Risling (2007) writes about the Hollywood scene:

> If a prescription needs to be filled in Hollywood, chances are celebrities can find a doctor to do it. Doctors have a long history of feeding the drug demands of the entertainment industry from Marilyn Monroe to Winona Ryder, Elvis Presley to Courtney Love. Now, California authorities are looking at a physician who reportedly prescribed methadone to Anna Nicole Smith under a fake name. The former Playboy Playmate died Feb. 8 after collapsing at a Florida hotel. The cause is under investigation.

Though research has yet to reveal what goes wrong when an OLL or OPL goes sour, it is evident that these lifestyles are no guarantee against sliding into serious negativeness. Yet it is also evident that positiveness is seldom as newsworthy as negativeness. Meanwhile, casual observation does suggest that far more people are happily cocooned in an OLL or OPL than not, for whom absorbing core activities leave little time or desire for negative pursuits, perhaps even for thinking about trying them.

Crime is another social problem where positive sociological principles may be able to play an ameliorative role. A major proportion of all crime is classified as some sort of property offense, and here change in the at-titude of property offenders, both free and serving sentences, might bear fruit. To understand this change we must return to our earlier discussion of money and simple living. There I cited Seligman's observation that "authentic happiness" comes from realizing our potential for enduring self-fulfillment. I argued next that such fulfillment is a cardinal reward of serious leisure, devotee work, and to some extent, project-based leisure. Then, based on what has been said throughout this book about fulfillment, I concluded it would be difficult to maintain that, for the most part, there is any direct link between it and money. After this I drew on the sociology of consumption as a partial explanation of this observation.

The goal of most property offenders is to make money, as by directly stealing it or by indirectly selling something they have stolen. They, too, want the good life that consumption appears to bring, evidence of which they see all around them. This is the attitude referred to in the preceding paragraph, and the one that positive sociology could help to change.

But is it not a tall order to try to convince the typical property offender to scale down his or her consumer goals and, as an alternative, find deep meaning and fulfillment and, eventually, well-being in complex leisure? Possibly, though to my knowledge, this approach has never been systematically tried. The challenge of changing the acquisitive orientation of these people would fall to the field of leisure education (chap. 4), which would need to develop instructional and counseling programs and techniques appropriate for prisoners, probationers, parolees, and where feasible, even practicing criminals. A leisure education program could be offered in parallel with an occupational training program (to the extent the latter exists).

A multitude of environmental issues have been defined as problematic by a huge variety of groups. The main way that leisure can help ameliorate any of them is by way of the efforts of environmental volunteers, whether career, casual, or project-based (see table 1.1). Environmental volunteering entails either monitoring or changing a particular set of external conditions affecting the people, flora, or fauna within their orbit. The change striven for is not always defined as favorable by everyone it concerns (e.g., mountain hikers might oppose a campaign by dirt-bikers' for new trails in areas where the former are benefiting from exclusive use). Career volunteering in the environmental sphere includes maintaining hiking trails and trout streams as well as creating, organizing and conducting environmentally related publicity campaigns (e.g., anti-smoking, clean air, potable water, anti-logging or mining, access to natural recreational resources including lakes, forests, ocean frontage). Any of these could also be pursued as leisure projects. The casual volunteer also finds opportunities in these examples, seen in door-to-door distribution of leaflets promoting a clean air campaign and picking up litter in a park or along a highway.

This is the main way. There are also subtler ways, however, which when practiced, amount to participation in the environmentalist social movement, a type of formation that is rapidly gaining momentum these days. All people in the community operating in all three domains of life assist it, or participate in it, when they intentionally refrain from littering, take public transit, use sparingly home heating and air conditioning, recycle cans and bottles, avoid dumping chemicals in the public sewerage system, and so on. Some day, perhaps, we will have research data showing precisely how positiveness is felt in these practices, since, depending on the situation, they may be defined as work or non-work obligation or as part of leisure. The latter is seen in packing out personal litter while hiking on public trails and working with friends to clean up refuse on an urban beach.

Conclusions

The risk in the preceding section of placing positive sociology in the role of helpmate for problem-centered sociology is, given the dominance of the latter in contemporary sociology, that scholars there might fail to appreciate the unique perspective of the former. This would be a shame. Its unique practical utility—as an approach to solving personal and social problems—is, I believe, well demonstrated in the preceding section. It is therefore time that sociology as a discipline recognizes the major role that positiveness has to play in the twenty-first century, wholeheartedly embrace this new field, and encourage further research and theory development in it.

Positive sociology rests on a distinctive combination of ideas, the most central being those composing the serious leisure perspective. The concepts of role, core activity, and general activity join with that of human agency in an explanation of how people become motivated to fashion their personal model of a worthwhile life in leisure and, for some of them, in leisure and devotee work. This they do within a great range of social and personal conditions which simultaneously frame, constrain, and facilitate positive activity in the domains of work and leisure. Some people are able to develop an optimal leisure or optimal positive lifestyle, which includes coming to grips with their unavoidable non-work obligations.

At present, we inhabit an exceedingly tumultuous world, nearly all of it made that way in one way or another by humans. The personal and social problems considered in this chapter are largely of our own doing as a species. Furthermore a significant portion of the tumult springs ultimately from people who have little or no stake in the status quo, for whom indeed the status quo is in some unavoidable way oppressive. Yet they see faint hope of escaping their lot.

In this chapter, we have explored some of the consequences of their situation, pointing out where positiveness in their lives could make a difference, could give them something worth living for. Positiveness can make present and future life more attractive and worthwhile than in the past. So, even if some people fail to gain a stake in the obligatory side of life (mainly nondevotee work), why not at minimum help them gain one in its positive side, in leisure (especially the serious and project-based forms) and, where possible, devotee work? I hope this book has shown just how profound and appealing the existence offered by these two domains can be to those who are willing and able to take advantage of their opportunities.

This book has concentrated, for the most part, on the three domains as experienced in the Western world. Yet readers may note that a substantial part of the tumult of our time—our current personal and social problems—comes from outside that region, while still undeniably affecting it. In this respect a couple of studies show that these words about positiveness may also be applied there. One reviews research showing that sport and recreation have been "proven" to be effective means for building peace in the Middle East (Jamieson & Ross, 2007). Competition is part of sport, but so also is cooperation, team building, positive identity, group empowerment, and similar positive processes. Along different but related lines Diener and Tov (2007) studied social well-being, finding that it varies widely across nations. They observed it was associated with, among other factors, confidence in government and the armed forces, emphasis on postmaterialist values, support for democracy, and lowered intolerance of immigrants and racial groups. An elevated sense of social well-being, the authors concluded, correlates strongly with peaceful attitudes. This is clearly an important area for further research.

Apart from a passing remark here and there, I have in this book ignored the impact of human agency on social change. This process has not escaped Chris Rojek (2000, pp. 19-20), however, who has underscored leisure's major contribution here. I now wish to add to his observation that, should we want to add more positiveness to people's lives or, if it is already there, to keep it from being eroded, we may occasionally have to change certain personal and social conditions or add them. Discovering which conditions to add or change to generate positiveness in which activities constitutes another cardinal research area for the new field.

Furthermore let us not forget our weak understanding of the domain of non-work obligation. This area is key because, by controlling if not reducing its demands, *homo otiosus* finds himself with more time for complex leisure and devotee work. But we sorely need research here on, for instance, the demographic variation in the nature and types of non-work obligations as well as on the meaning of such activity for those faced with doing it. A decent history of this domain would also be invaluable.

All this shows why the present book must be viewed as a foundational treatise on a positive sociology. It is a presentation of the basic concepts and propositions that I believe compose its essence. Some of these concepts and propositions may seem novel, even if in fact, all have been drawn from pertinent areas of sociology, psychology, social psychology, leisure studies, and a few other fields. In this way I hope to have established a base for further theoretical and empirical work in this new field as well as justified placing it at the top of the list of "must do" projects for sociology in the West.

There has never been a better time in history than now for accentuating the positive. Here sociology should be leading the charge. Thích Nhat Hanh, Vietnamese Buddhist monk, poet, and peacemaker, holds that "people deal too much with the negative, with what is wrong. Why not try and see positive things, to just touch those things and make them bloom" (source unknown)? I agree. And this book offers a way of seeing and pursuing that which makes life worth living, a way of creating a worthwhile existence that is, in combination, rewarding, satisfying, and fulfilling.

Notes

1.   I am indebted to Paul Burns, University of Bedfordshire, for bringing to my attention this unusual, but well-established, kind of work and leisure.
2.   Among the books see, for instance, M.P. Dunleavey, *Money Can Buy Happiness: How to Spend to Get the Life You Want* (2007); L. Rowley, *Money and Happiness: A Guide to Living the Good Life* (2005); H.S. Brock, *Your Complete Guide to Money Happiness: How to Achieve Financial Success, Security, and Peace of Mind* (1997).
3.   One of my respondents in the baseball study (Stebbins, 1979) actually said as much, though he said he loved his girlfriend more than he loved football (which he did not play). He did not seem to be joking.
4.   Remember that some exercise activities may be defined as disagreeable obligation (chap. 1).

References

Applebaum, H. (1992). *The concept of work: Ancient, medieval, and modern.* Albany: State University of New York Press.

Arai, S.M., & Pedlar, A.M. (1997). Building Communities through leisure: Citizen participation in a healthy communities initiative. *Journal of Leisure Research*, 29, 167-182.

Aronowitz, S., & DiFazio, W. (1994). *The jobless future: Sci-tech and the dogma of work.* Minneapolis: University of Minnesota Press.

Baldwin, C.K., & Norris, P.A. (1999). Exploring the dimensions of serious leisure: Love me—love my dog. *Journal of Leisure Research*, 31, 1-17.

Bandura , A. (1989a). Human agency in social cognitive theory. *American Psychologist*, 44, 1175-1184.

Bandura, A. (1989b). Regulation of cognitive processes through perceived self-efficacy, *Developmental Psychology*, 25, 729-735.

Bandura, A. (1997). *Self-efficacy: The exercise of control.* New York: Freeman.

Bartram, S.A. (2001). Serious leisure careers among whitewater kayakers: A feminist perspective, *World Leisure Journal*, 43(2), 4-11.

Beck, U. (2000). *The brave new world of work,* trans. by P. Camiller. New York: Polity Press.

Blackshaw, T., & Long, J. (1998). A critical examination of the advantages of investigating community and leisure from a social network perspective. *Leisure Studies*, 17, 233-248.

Boesveld, S. (2007). Doctor burnout hurts health care. *Calgary Herald*, Wednesday 3 October.

Bott, E. (1957). *Family and social network.* London, UK: Tavistock Publications.

Bowen, C.D. (1935). *Friends and fiddlers.* Boston, MA: Little Brown.

Braverman, H. (1974). *Labor and monopoly capital: The degradation of work in the twentieth century.* New York: Monthly Review Press.

Brissett, D., & Snow, R.P. (1993). Boredom: Where the future isn't. *Symbolic Interaction*, 16, 237-256.

Brightbill, C.K. (1961). *Man and leisure: A philosophy of recreation.* Englewood Cliffs, NJ: Prentice-Hall.

Brooks, D. (2007). The odyssey years. *New York Times*, 9 October (online edition).

Bush, D.M., & Simmons, R.G. (1990). Socialization processes over the life course. In M. Rosenberg & R.H. Turner (Eds.), *Social Psychology* (pp. 133-164). New Brunswick, NJ: Transaction Publishers.

Butler, R.N. (1963). The life review: An interpretation of reminiscence in the aged. *Psychiatry*, 26, 65-76.

Campbell, A., Converse, P., & Rogers, W.L. (1976). *The quality of American life: Perceptions, evaluations, and satisfactions.* New York: Russell Sage Foundation.

Cohen, J. (2002). *Protestantism and capitalism: The mechanisms of influence.* New York: Aldine de Gruyter.

Cohen-Gewerc, E., & Stebbins, R.A. (Eds.) (2007). *The Pivotal Role of Leisure Education: Finding Personal-Fulfillment in This Century.* State College, PA: Venture.

Commonwealth Secretariat (2007). *Civil paths to peace: Report of the Commonwealth Commission on respect and Understanding.* London.

Cross, G. (1990). *A social history of leisure since 1600.* State College, PA: Venture.

Cross, G, & Logemann, J. (2004). Home improvement. In G. Cross (Ed.), *Encyclopedia of recreation and leisure in America* (pp. 447-449). Detroit, MI: Thomson/Gale.

Csikszentmihalyi, M. (1990). *Flow: The psychology of optimal experience.* New York: Harper & Row.

Cuskelly, G., & Harrington, M. (1997). Volunteers and leisure: Evidence of marginal and career volunteerism in sport. *World Leisure & Recreation,* 39 (3), 11-18.

Darley, J. M., & Latané, B. (1968). Bystander intervention in emergencies: Diffusion of responsibility. *Journal of Personality and Social Psychology,* 8, 377-383.

Dattilo, J., & Murphy, W.D. (1991). *Leisure education program planning: A systematic approach.* State College, PA: Venture.

DeMuth, D.H. (2004). Another look at resilience: Challenging the stereotypes of aging. *Journal of Feminist Family Therapy,* 16, 61-74.

Desmond, A., & Moore, J. (1991). *Darwin.* London: Michael Joseph.

Diener, E., & Tov, W. (2007). Subjective Well-Being and Peace. *Journal of Social Issues,* 63, 421-440.

Doohan, L. (1990). *Leisure: A spiritual need.* Notre Dame, IN: Ave Maria Press.

Dubin, R. (1979). Central life interests: Self-integrity in a complex world. *Pacific Sociological Review,* 22, 404-426.

Duval, D.T. (2003). Anthropology. In J.M. Jenkins & J.J. Pigram (Eds.), *Encyclopedia of leisure and outdoor recreation* (pp. 16-19). London: Routledge.

The Economist (2005). Up off the couch. 22 October, p. 35.

The Economist (2006). The land of pleasure. 2 February (WWW.Economist.com).

The Economist (2007a). Where money seems to talk. 14 July, pp. 63-64.

The Economist (2007b). To avoid the big C, stay small. 3 November, pp. 93-94.

Elgin, D. (1981). *Voluntary simplicity: Toward a way of life that is outwardly simple, inwardly rich.* New York: William Morrow.

Fisher, B., Day, M., & Collier, C. (1998). Successful aging: Volunteerism and generativity in later life. In D. Redburn & R, McNamara (Eds.), *Social gerontology* (pp. 43-54). Westport, CT: Auburn.

Florida, R. (2002). *The rise of the creative class and how it's transforming work, leisure, community, and everyday life.* New York: Basic Books.

Fullagar, S., & Owler, K. (1998). Narratives of leisure: Recreating the self. *Disability and Society,* 13, 441-450.

Gagnon, J.H., & Simon, W. (2005). *Sexual conduct: The sources of human sexuality,* 2nd ed. New Brunswick, NJ : Transaction Publishers.

Gelber, S.M. (1999). *Hobbies: Leisure and the culture of work in America.* New York: Columbia University Press.

Gerth, Hans and Mills, C. Wright (Eds.) (1958). *From Max Weber: Essays in Sociology.* New York: Oxford University Press.

Gini, A. (2001). *My self, my job: Work and the creation of the modern individual.* New York: Routledge.

Goff, S.J., Fick, D.S., & Oppliger, R.A. (1997). The moderating effect of spouse support on the relation between serious leisure and spouses' perceived leisure-family conflict. *Journal of Leisure Research,* 29, 47-60.

Goffman, E. (1963). *Stigma: Notes on the management of spoiled identity.* Englewood Cliffs, NJ: Prentice-Hall.

Greenwald, M. (2008). The comprehensive exit plan (manuscript).

Hamel, J. (2003). *Swinging: A societal phenomenon (Québec edition)*, trans. by D. C. Gordon. Greenfield Park, QC: Editions CÉQSC.

Hamilton-Smith, E. (1995). The connexions of scholarship. *Newsletter* (Official newsletter of RC13 of the International Sociological Association), March, 4-9.

Hamilton-Smith, E. (2003). History. In J.M. Jenkins & J.J. Pigram (Eds.), *Encyclopedia of leisure and outdoor recreation* (pp. 225-228). London: Routledge.

Harrison, J. (2001). Thinking about tourists. *International Sociology, 16*, 159-172.

Hartmann, D., & Massoglia, M. (2007). Reassessing the relationship between high school sports participation and deviance: Evidence of enduring, bifurcated effects. *The Sociological Quarterly*, 48, 485-505.

Hastings, D.W., Kurth, S.B., & Schloder, M. (1996). Work routines in the serious leisure career of Canadian and U.S. masters swimmers. *Avanté*, 2, 73-92.

Havner, R. (2007). Begging for teachers, many say, "I quit," and "crisis" may be looming. *Mobile Press-Register* 15 July (electronic edition).

Haworth, J.T. (1986). Meaningful activity and psychological models of non-employment. *Leisure Studies*, 5, 281-297.

Haworth, J.T. (2004). Enjoyment and well-being. In J.T. Haworth (Ed.), *Work, leisure and well-being* (pp. 83-102). London: Routledge.

Haworth, J.T., & Hill, S. (1992). Work, leisure, and psychological well-being in a sample of young adults. *Journal of Community & Applied Social Psychology*, 2, 147-160.

Helft, M. (2007). With tools on Web, amateurs reshape mapmaking *New York Times*, 27 July (online edition).

Hemingway, J. L. (1999). Leisure, social capital, and democratic citizenship. *Journal of Leisure Research*, 31, 150-165.

Heuser, L. (2005). We're not too old to play sports: The career of women lawn bowlers. *Leisure Studies*, 24, 45-60.

Homer-Dixon, T. (2007). A swiftly melting planet. *New York Times*, Thursday, 4 Oct (online edition).

Houle, C.O. (1961). *The inquiring mind*. Madison: University of Wisconsin Press.

Huizinga, J. (1955). *Homo ludens: A study of the play element in culture*. Boston, MA: Beacon.

Iso-Ahola, S. (1997). A psychological analysis of leisure and health. In J.T. Haworth (Ed.), *Work, leisure and well-being* (pp. 131-144). London: Routledge.

Iso-Ahola, S.E., & Crowley, E.D. (1991) Adolsecent substance abuse and leisure boredom. *Journal of Leisure Research*, 23, 260-271.

Jamieson, L.M., & Ross, C.M. (2007). Using recreation to curb extremism. *Parks & Recreation*, 42 (2), 26-29.

Jarvis, P. (1995). *Adult and continuing education* (2nd ed.). London, UK: Routledge.

Jeffries, V., Johnston, B.V., Nichols, L.T., Oliner, S.P., Tiryakian, E, & Weinstein, J. (2006). *Altruism and social solidarity: Envisioning a field of specialization. American Sociologist* , 37 (3), 67-83.

Jones, I., & Symon, G. (2001). Lifelong learning as serious leisure: Policy, practice, and potential. *Leisure Studies*, 20, 269-284.

Kalleberg, A.L. (2007). *The mismatched worker.* New York: W.W. Norton.

Kane, M. (2007). Few believe they can balance work, life. *Calgary Herald*, Wednesday, 25 April, p. A11.

Kaplan, M. (1960). *Leisure in America: A social inquiry*. New York: John Wiley.

Kay, T. (1990). Active unemployment - A leisure pattern for the future. *Loisir et Société/ Society and Leisure*, 12, 413-430.

Keen, A. (2007). *The cult of the amateur: How today's internet is killing our culture.* New York: Doubleday/Currency.

Kelly, J.R. (1990). *Leisure*, 2ⁿᵈ ed. Englewood Cliffs, NJ: Prentice-Hall.

Keyes, C.L.M. (1998). Social well-being. *Social Psychology Quarterly*, 61, 121-140.

Killinger, B. (1997). *Workaholism: The respectable addicts*. Toronto. ON: Firefly Books.

Lambdin, L. (1997). *Elderlearning*. Phoenix, AZ: Oryx Press.

Laslett, P. (1994). The third age, the fourth age and the future. *Aging and Society*, 14, 436-447.

Layard, R. (2005). *Happiness: Lessons from a new science*. New York: Penguin.

Leadbeater, C., & Miller, P. (2004). *The pro-am revolution: How enthusiasts are changing our economy and society*. London, UK: Demos.

Leitner, M.J. & Leitner S.F. (1994). *How to improve your life through leisure*. Salt Lake City, UT: Northwest Publishing.

Leitner, M.J., & Leitner, S.F. (2004). *Leisure enhancement*, 3rd ed. New York: Haworth.

Levine, P. (2007). *The future of democracy: Developing the next generation of American citizens*. Medford, MA: Tufts University Press.

Luft, C.A. (2007). Meeting online friends: Personal relationships in the 21ˢᵗ century. Masters Thesis, Department of Sociology, University of Calgary.

Lyons, K., & Dionigi, R. (2007). Transcending emotional community: A qualitative examination of older adults and Masters' sports participation. *Leisure Sciences*, 29, 375-389.

Machlowitz, M. (1980). *Workaholics: Living with them, working with them*. Reading, MA: Addison-Wesley.

Maffesoli, M. (1996). *The time of the tribes: The decline of individualism*, trans. by D. Smith. London: Sage Publications.

Mannell, R.C. (1993). High investment activity and life satisfaction among older adults: Committed, serious leisure, and flow activities. In J.R. Kelly (Ed.), *Activity and aging: Staying involved in later life* (pp.125-145). Newbury Park, CA: Sage.

Manning, P.K. (1999). High-risk narratives: Textual adventures. *Qualitative Sociology*, 22, 285-299.

McBrearty, S., & Stringer, C. (2007). The coast in colour. *Nature*, 449 (18 October), 793-794.

McCall, G.J., & Simmons, J.L. (1978). *Identities and interactions*, rev. ed. New York: Free Press.

McQuarrie, F., & Jackson, E.L. (1996). Connections between negotiation of leisure constraints and serious leisure: An exploratory study of adult amateur ice skaters. *Loisir et Société/Society and Leisure*, 19, 459-483.

Mead, G.H. (1934). *Mind, self, and society* (C.W. Morris, Ed.). Chicago, IL: University of Chicago Press.

Mellor, B. E. (2006). Radical shift: A grounded theory approach to midlife career change of professionals. Masters Thesis, Department of Sociology, University of Calgary.

Muñoz, S.S. (2006). In clubs and online, hobbyists embrace the joys of picking. *Wall Street Journal*, Saturday/Sunday (28 October), p. A1.

Nazareth, L. (2007). *The leisure economy: How changing demographics, economics, and generational attitudes will reshape our lives and our industries*. Mississauga, ON: John Wiley & Sons Canada.

Oatley, K., Keltner, D., & Jenkins, J.J. (2006). *Understanding emotions,* 2nd ed. Malden, MA: Blackwell.

Olson, E.G. (2006). *Personal development and discovery through leisure*, 3rd ed. Dubuque, IA: Kendall/Hunt.

Orthner, D.K. (1975). Leisure activity patterns and marital satisfaction over the marital career. *Journal of Marriage and the Family*, 37, 91-104.

Oswald, A.J., & Powdthavee, N. (2007). Review 1: Obesity, unhappiness, and the challenge of affluence: theory and evidence, *Economic Journal*, 117, 441-454.

Ouellette, P. (2003). L'application de la spiritualité bénédictine au loisir des personnes âgées: Une formulation théorique du bonheur spirituel. Moncton, NB : École de kinésiologie et récréologie, Université de Moncton. Retrieved 14 December 2005, from http://catalogue.iugm.qc.ca/Auteur.htm?numrec=061904268918600

Ouellette, P., & Carette, P. (2004). Les motivations et les effets d'une retraite individuelle dans un monastère bénédictin. Moncton, NB : Ecole de kinésiologie et de récréologie, Université de Moncton.

Parker, S. (1983). *Leisure and work*. London: George Allen & Unwin.

Patterson, I., Pegg, S., & Dobson-Patterson, R. (2000). Exploring the links between leisure boredom and alcohol use among youth in rural and urban areas of Australia. *Journal of Parks and Recreation Administration*, 18 (3), 53-75.

Pearce, J.L. (1993). *Volunteers: The organizational behavior of unpaid workers*, London: Routledge.

Principal Financial Services (2004). The principal global financial well-being survey: 2004 executive summary. Des Moines, IA: Principal Life Insurance Co.

Putnam, R.D. (2000). *Bowling alone: The collapse and revival of American community*. New York: Simon & Schuster.

Rapoport, R.N., & Rapoport, R. (1975). *Leisure and the family life cycle*. London, UK: Routledge & Kegan Paul.

Reid, D. (1995). Work and leisure in the 21st century: From production to citizenship. Toronto: Wall and Emerson.

Reiss, R. L. (1986). *Journey into sexuality: An exploratory voyage*. Englewood Cliffs, NJ: Prentice-Hall.

Ridgeway CL. (1994). Affect. In *Group Processes*: *Sociological Analyses*, ed. M Foschi, EJ Lawler, pp. 205–30. Chicago: Nelson-Hall.

Riesman, D. (1961). *The lonely crowd: A study of the changing American character* (rev. ed.). New Haven, CT: Yale University Press.

Rifkin, J. (1995). *The end of work: The decline of the global labor force and the dawn of the post-market era*. New York, NY: G.P. Putnam's Sons.

Risling, G. (2007). Prescription drugs part of Hollywood. *ABC News Internet Ventures* (retrieved 7 October 2007).

Roberson, D.N., Jr. (2005). Leisure and learning: An investigation of older adults and self-directed learning. *Leisure/Loisir*, 29, 203-238.

Rojek, C. (1997). Leisure theory: Retrospect and prospect. *Loisir et Société/Society and Leisure*, 20, 383-400.

Rojek, C. (2000). *Leisure and culture*. Houndmills, Hampshire: Palgrave.

Rojek, C. (2002). Civil labour, leisure and post work society. *Loisir et Société/Society and Leisure*, 25, 21-36.

Rosenberg, B., & Fliegel, N. (1965). *The vanguard artist: Portrait and self-portrait*. Chicago: Quadrangle.

Rotter, J.B. (1990). Internal versus external locus of control of reinforcement: A case history of a variable. *American Psychologist*, 45 (4), 489-493.

Rushe, D. (2007). "Workaholism" epidemic goes global. *Calgary Herald*, Sunday 10 June, p. D4.

Seeman, M. (1972). Alienation and engagement. In A. Campbell & P.E. Converse (Eds.), *The human meaning of social change* (pp. 467-527). New York: Russell Sage Foundation.

Seligman, M.E.P. (2003). *Authentic happiness: Using the new positive psychology to realize your potential for lasting fulfillment*. New York: Free Press.

Seligman, M.E.P., & Csikszentmihalyi, M. (2000). Positive psychology: An introduction. *American Psychologist*, 55(1), 5-14.

Selman, G., Cooke, M., Selman, M., & Dampier, P. (1998). *The foundations of adult education in Canada* (2nd ed.). Toronto, ON: Thompson Educational Publishing.

Silverberg, S. (2007). Employee perceptions of organizational commitment: An exploratory study. Ph.D. Dissertation, Department of Sociology, University of Calgary.

Silverman, M.A. (2006). Beyond fun in games: The serious leisure of the power gamer. Masters Dissertation, Department of Sociology, Concordia University.

Slevin, J. (2007). Internet. In G. Ritzer (Ed.), *The Blackwell encyclopedia of sociology*, vol. 5 (pp. 2384-3288. Malden, MA: Blackwell.

Smith, D.H. (2000). *Grassroots associations*. Thousand Oaks, CA: Sage Publications.

Smith, D.H., Stebbins, R.A., & M. Dover (2006). *A dictionary of nonprofit terms and concepts*. Bloomington: Indiana University Press.

Snyder, C.R., & Lopez, J. (2007). *Positive psychology: The scientific and practical explorations of human strengths*. Thousand Oaks, CA: Sage.

Sonnenberg, R. (1996). *Living with workaholism*. St. Louis, MO: Concordia Publishing House.

Spector, M, & Kitsuse, J.L. (1987). *Constructing social problems*, 2nd ed. Menlo Park, CA: Cummings.

Stalp, M.C. (2006). Negotiating time and space for serious leisure: Quilting in the modern U.S. home. *Journal of Leisure Research*, 38, 104-132.

Stebbins, R.A. (1970). Career: The subjective approach. *Sociological Quarterly*, 11, 32-49.

Stebbins, R.A. (1976). Music among friends: The social networks of amateur musicians. *International Review of Sociology* (Series II), 12 (April-August), pp. 52-73.

Stebbins, R.A. (1979). *Amateurs: On the margin between work and leisure*. Beverly Hills, CA: Sage.

Stebbins, R.A. (1981). The social psychology of selfishness. *Canadian Review of Sociology and Anthropology*, 18, 82-92.

Stebbins, R.A. (1982). Serious leisure: A conceptual statement. *Pacific Sociological Review*, 25, 251-272.

Stebbins, R.A. (1992). *Amateurs, professionals, and serious leisure*. Montreal, QC and Kingston, ON: McGill-Queen's University Press.

Stebbins, R.A. (1993). *Canadian football. A view from the helmet.* (reprinted ed.). Toronto, ON: Canadian Scholars Press.

Stebbins, R.A. (1994). The liberal arts hobbies: A neglected subtype of serious leisure. *Loisir et Société/Society and Leisure*,16, 173-186.

Stebbins, R.A. (1995). Leisure and selfishness: An exploration. In G. S. Fain (Ed.), *Reflections on the philosophy of leisure, Vol. II, Leisure and ethics* (pp. 292-303). Reston, VA: American Alliance for Health, Physical Education, Recreation, and Dance.

Stebbins, R.A. (1996a). *The barbershop singer: Inside the social world of a musical hobby*. Toronto, ON: University of Toronto Press.

Stebbins, R.A. (1996b). *Tolerable differences: Living with deviance* (2nd ed). Toronto, ON: McGraw-Hill Ryerson.

Stebbins, R.A. (1996c). Volunteering: A serious leisure perspective. *Nonprofit and Voluntary Sector Quarterly*, 25, 211-224.

Stebbins, R.A. (1997a). Casual leisure: A conceptual statement. *Leisure Studies*, 16, 17-25.

Stebbins, R.A. (1997b). Lifestyle as a generic concept in ethnographic research. *Quality & Quantity*, 31, 347-360.

Stebbins, R.A. (1998a). *After work: The search for an optimal leisure lifestyle*. Calgary, AB: Detselig.

Stebbins, R.A. (1998b). *The urban francophone volunteer: Searching for personal meaning and community growth in a linguistic minority.* Vol. 3, No. 2 (New Scholars-New Visions in Canadian Studies quarterly monographs series). Seattle: University of Washington, Canadian Studies Centre.

Stebbins, R.A. (2000a). Obligation as an aspect of leisure experience. *Journal of Leisure Research*, 32, 152-155.

Stebbins , R. A. (2000b). Optimal leisure lifestyle: Combining serious and casual leisure for personal well-being. In M. C. Cabeza (Ed.), *Leisure and human development: Proposals for the 6th World Leisure Congress.* (pp. 101-107). Bilbao, Spain: University of Deusto.

Stebbins, R.A. (2001a). *New directions in the theory and research of serious leisure.* Mellen Studies in Sociology, vol. 28. Lewiston, NY: Edwin Mellen.

Stebbins, R. A. (2001b). Volunteering—mainstream and marginal: Preserving the leisure experience. In M. Graham & M. Foley (Eds.), *Volunteering in leisure: Marginal or inclusive?* (Vol. 75, pp. 1-10). Eastbourne, UK: Leisure Studies Association.

Stebbins, R.A. (2001c). The costs and benefits of hedonism: Some consequences of taking casual leisure seriously. *Leisure Studies*, 20, 305-309.

Stebbins, R. A. (2002). *The organizational basis of leisure participation: A motivational exploration.* State College, PA: Venture Publishing.

Stebbins, R.A. (2003). Boredom in free time. *Leisure Studies Association Newsletter*, 64 (March), 29-31. (also available at www.soci.ucalgary.ca/seriousleisure—Digital Library)

Stebbins, R.A. (2004a). *Between work and leisure: The common ground of two separate worlds.* New Brunswick, NJ: Transaction Publishers.

Stebbins, R.A. (2004b). Pleasurable aerobic activity: A type of casual leisure with salubrious implications. *World Leisure Journal*, 46(4), 55-58.

Stebbins, R.A. (2004c). Fun, enjoyable, satisfying, fulfilling: Describing positive leisure experience. *Leisure Studies Association Newsletter*, 69 (November), 8-11. (also available at www.soci.ucalgary.ca/seriousleisure—Digital Library)

Stebbins, R.A. (2005a). Choice and experiential definitions of leisure. *Leisure Sciences*, 27, 349-352.

Stebbins, R.A. (2005b). *Challenging mountain nature: Risk, motive, and lifestyle in three hobbyist sports.* Calgary, AB: Detselig.

Stebbins, R.A. (2005c). Project-based leisure: Theoretical neglect of a common use of free time. *Leisure Studies*, 24, 1-11.

Stebbins, R.A. (2006a). *Serious leisure: A perspective for our time.* New Brunswick, NJ: Transaction Publishers.

Stebbins, R.A. (2006b). Leisure Lifestyles. In R.E. McCarville & K.J. MacKay (Eds.), *Leisure for Canadians* (pp. 51-58). State College, PA: Venture.

Stebbins, R.A. (2006c). Mentoring as a leisure activity: On the informal world of small-scale altruism. *World Leisure Journal*, 48 (4), 3-10.

Stebbins, R.A. (2006d). Contemplation as leisure and nonleisure. *Leisure Studies Association Newsletter*, 73 (March), 21-23. (also available at www.soci.ucalgary.ca/seriousleisure—Digital Library)

Stebbins, R.A. (2007a). The sociology of entertainment. In C.D. Bryant & D.L. Peck (Eds.), *The Handbook of 21st Century Sociology* (178-185, chap. 21). Thousand Oaks, CA: Sage.

Stebbins, R.A. (2007b). A leisure-based, theoretic typology of volunteers and volunteering. *Leisure Studies Association Newsletter*, 78 (November), XX . (also available at www.soci.ucalgary.ca/seriousleisure—Digital Library)

Stebbins, R.A. (2007c). Leisure studies: The happy science. *Leisure Studies Association Newsletter*, 76 (March), 20-22. (also available at www.soci.ucalgary.ca/seriousleisure—Digital Library)

Stebbins, (2007d). Les Frontières entre les loisirs et le travail : Cinq ponts. Reference to follow.

Stebbins, R.A. (2008a). The leisure basis of caring. *Leisure Studies Association Newsletter*, 79 (March), XX. (also available at www.soci.ucalgary.ca/seriousleisure—Digital Library)

Stebbins, R.A. (2008b). Leisure and consumption: Not always the same." In J. Caudwell, S. Redhead, & A. Tomlinson (Eds.). Relocating the leisure society: Media, consumption and spaces (LSA Publication No. 101) (pp. 67-76). Eastbourne, UK: Leisure Studies Association.

Stebbins, R.A. (in press). Right leisure: Serious, casual, or project-based? *NeuroRehabilitation*

Sylvester, C. (1999). The Western idea of work and leisure: Traditions, transformations, and the future. In E.L. Jackson and T.L. Burton (Eds.), *Leisure studies: Prospects for the twenty-first century* (pp. 17-34). State College, PA: Venture.

Tanquerey, A. A. (1924). *Précis de théologie ascétique et mystique.* Paris : Desclé.

Taylor, C. (1991). *The malaise of modernity.* Toronto, ON: The House of Anancy Press.

Turner, J.H., & Stets, J.E. (2006). Sociological theories of human emotions. In K.S. Cook & D.S. Massey (Eds.), *Annual Review of Sociology*, vol. 32, pp. 25-52. Palo Alto, CA: Annual Reviews.

UNESCO. (1976). Recommendation on the development of adult education. Paris, France.

Unruh, D.R. (1979). Characteristics and types of participation in social worlds. *Symbolic Interaction*, 2, 115-130.

Unruh, D.R. (1980). The nature of social worlds. *Pacific Sociological Review*, 23, 271-296.

Veal, A.J. (1993). The concept of lifestyle: A review. *Leisure Studies*, 12, 233-252.

Van den Hoonaard, W.C. (1997). *Working with sensitizing concepts: Analytical field research* (Qualitative Research Methods Series 41). Thousand Oaks, CA: Sage.

Warr, P. (1987). *Work, unemployment and mental health.* Oxford, UK: Clarendon.

Wearing, B., & Fulager, S. (1996). The ambiguity in Australian women's family leisure: Some figures and refiguring. In N Samuel (Ed.), *Women, leisure and the family in contemporary society: A multinational Perspective* (pp. 15-34). Wallingford, Oxon, UK: CABI Publishing.

Weber, M. (1947). *The theory of social and economic organization*, trans. by T. Parsons. New York: The Free Press.

Wilkins, S. (2001). Aging, chronic illness and self-concept: A study of women with osteoporosis. *Journal of Women and Aging*, 13, 73-92.

Williams, R.M., Jr. (2000). American society. In E.F. Borgatta, & R.J.V. Montgomery (Eds.), *Encyclopedia of sociology*, 2nd ed., Vol. 1 (pp. 140-148). New York: Macmillan.

Wuthnow, R. (1991). *Acts of compassion: Caring for others and helping ourselves.* Princeton, NJ: Princeton University Press.

Wuthnow, R. (2007). *After the baby boomers: How the twenty- and thirty-somethings are shaping the future of American religion.* Princeton, NJ: Princeton University Press.

Index